IMAGES
of America

WESTERN NEW YORK
STEEL

The Lackawanna Building, more commonly known as the "North" or "Old Main" Office Building, is seen here shortly after its construction in 1901. It was designed by renowned architect L.C. Holden in the Beaux Arts style. The facade was constructed of white sandstone, and the roof was lined with copper, complete with laurel-wreath dormer windows and lion heads. Office staff was relocated from Scranton, Pennsylvania, and took up residence here on September 30, 1901. The Administration Building in Lackawanna became the symbolic embodiment of Western New York's steel industry, from its construction as an architectural masterpiece to its slow decline over the course of the 20th century. The building was demolished in 2013 in the wake of a very public legal battle splitting the community on the issue of historic preservation. (Courtesy of the Steel Plant Museum of Western New York.)

ON THE COVER: Taken on November 9, 1956, this photograph shows a furnace in No. 1 open-hearth shop "tapping" steel into ladle No. 6 at Bethlehem Steel Company's Lackawanna plant. Tapping refers to the process of drilling a hole into the back of the hearth, releasing molten steel. (Courtesy of the Steel Plant Museum of Western New York.)

IMAGES
of America

WESTERN NEW YORK
STEEL

Spencer D. Morgan

ARCADIA
PUBLISHING

Published by Arcadia Publishing
Charleston, South Carolina

Library of Congress Control Number: 2013941302

For all general information, please contact Arcadia Publishing:
Telephone 843-853-2070
Fax 843-853-0044
E-mail sales@arcadiapublishing.com
For customer service and orders:
Toll-Free 1-888-313-2665

Visit us on the Internet at www.arcadiapublishing.com

To Mel and Peggy Pawlak:
Your strength and perseverance inspired this book.
Your dedication and support continues to inspire its author.

CONTENTS

Acknowledgments   6

Introduction   7

1.   Location, Location, Location   11

2.   Shipping and Transportation   25

3.   Made in the USA   41

4.   Life Inside the Plant   55

5.   A Community of Steel   67

6.   Labor Relations   79

7.   Steel and War   93

8.   Tightening the Rust Belt   105

Bibliography   126

About the Steel Plant Museum of Western New York   127

ACKNOWLEDGMENTS

Inspiration is at the heart of every work. This book would not have been possible if it had not been for the community of Western New York, from the volunteers at the local museums to the last-generation steelworkers whose experiences and stories are important to the legacy of this region's past, present, and future.

Thank you to Ron Dukarm and the rest of the volunteers at the Western New York Railway Historical Society (WNYRHS). The region's steel and rail history will forever be intertwined. One story cannot be told without the other.

At the Historical Society of the Tonawandas, thank you to Carole Barnard. Your help with the Tonawanda Iron & Steel Company research helped make this book more inclusive.

Thank you to Cynthia Van Ness and the Buffalo History Museum. Our community will forever be indebted to this organization for so many reasons. Thank you for the help researching the area's earliest smithies and iron forges.

The Steel Plant Museum of Western New York (SPMWNY) is largely responsible for the inspiration of this book. Most of the images and histories have come out of SPMWNY's archives. Unless otherwise noted, all images appear courtesy of the Steel Plant Museum of Western New York.

Thank you to the numerous SPMWNY volunteers, members, and donors who contributed to this book. Special thanks to the keepers of the flame: Mike Malyak, Don Williams, Melvin and Marguerite Pawlak, Chesterine (Evanisko) Gorman, Angie Yelich, Daniel and Gloria Tomaszewski, Joyce Walker, Edward "Doug" Bender, Jim Torgeson, Everett and Roxanne Bennett, Jerry and Lorraine Soltis, Erica Wanecski, Mary Ann Turkla, Melody Bus, James Carey Jr., and Bridget Quinn-Carey, Barbara Kuzina, Romaine Lillis, Bob Stevens, and all the rest at SPMWNY. The entire region appreciates your gracious dedication and support in keeping this history alive. The stories and experiences you have shared have brought meaning and understanding to this endeavor.

Finally, thank you to Dennis and Eileen Morgan, Scott Morgan, Jason and Heather Billings, Rachel Morgan, Phil and Sharon Blair, and the rest of the author's family and friends who have supported his efforts and have helped make this book possible.

INTRODUCTION

The purpose of this book is to identify the steel industry that influenced the transformation of the Western New York region. For more than 200 years, iron and steel have been hammered, smelted, molded, cast, and rolled in Buffalo and the surrounding area. Hundreds of companies brought the clamor, grime, and smoke of the steel industry to the region's back door. Hundreds of thousands of men and women were employed by the industry, while other businesses and services benefited from the commerce they brought. Likewise, many more would suffer the unemployment and exodus that occurred throughout Western New York as the industry collapsed.

So many companies were formed and so many businesses remain despite the Rust Belt economic climate. Unfortunately, not every manufacturer could be mentioned or shown in this book. The author deeply apologizes for any company that might have been overlooked or has simply gone unmentioned. Most of these images show workers at the Bethlehem Steel plant in Lackawanna and the Republic Steel plant in Buffalo. However, there are so many wonderful stories to be told about the steel industry in Western New York. From Dunkirk to Olean to Lockport and everywhere in between, this region benefited a great deal from the steel companies that were established here. So many people were affected by the loss of these companies. Although the community of Western New York is still struggling to overcome its own deindustrialization, there is a glimmer of hope. Buffalo has seen its dark age, and a renaissance has already begun to transform the Queen City and the surrounding region once again.

This book focuses on the rise and decline of Western New York's steel industry throughout the 20th century, from 1900 to approximately 1982. To understand the events that took place then, it is important to look at the history of the industry leading up to the year 1900. The steel industry in Western New York traces its roots back to the first blacksmiths who came to the area. Before 1800, there are little to no records of early smithies being built in the region, although it is more than likely that iron working did take place during the French and English colonial periods. In 1803, the first documented blacksmith in Erie County settled in Clarence. That same year, David Reese became the first blacksmith to arrive in Buffalo, then known as the village of New Amsterdam. He came to the area to teach the local native tribes the blacksmithing trade. In 1806, Reese built a smithy on the corner of what are now Seneca and Washington Streets in downtown Buffalo. His shop was one of only a handful of buildings to survive the 1813 burning of Buffalo by the British, and was used for almost 20 years.

By 1825, a total of 17 men were employed by seven smithies in Buffalo, with many more scattered around the surrounding countryside. As farming and trade villages began to spring up throughout the Western New York region, rural blacksmiths began to set up shop. Some farmers even practiced the trade themselves as an additional asset to the daily operation of their homesteads.

On November 4, 1825, the first boats from Buffalo entered New York Harbor via the Erie Canal; Western New York would never be the same. Within a few months, Edward Root established the first foundry in Buffalo, manufacturing plow irons and other basic tools. Five more, all constructed in Black Rock, would follow him. Black Rock was then a rival canal terminus and was not annexed by Buffalo until the 1850s. Although a few foundries were constructed in and around Buffalo, Black Rock was the iron and steel manufacturing center during the region's canal period.

The first forge was built at Black Rock Dam in 1838. A rolling mill was constructed in 1846 known as Buffalo Iron & Nail Works. This company would become Pratt & Company, and then the Pratt & Letchworth Company. This mill was the forerunner of Western New York's iron and steel industry in the 1800s and a precursor to what came in the next century. In 1864, Pratt & Company built the first blast furnace. By the 1880s, it employed almost 800 men. In 1888, Pratt & Letchworth was the first company to use open-hearth manufacturing in the region.

In the years leading up to the Civil War, the steel industry in Western New York was scarce, with the exception of a handful of ironworks and foundries. By 1864, more than 20 machine shops and other basic iron-production companies were established, in addition to those already in operation throughout the region.

In the years during and after the Civil War, Buffalo became a booming trade city. The postwar years ushered in an age of industrial expansion. A number of foundries, forges, and engineering plants sprang up throughout the region. The steam engine offered more efficient transportation of goods and services, advancements in rails and shipping overcame trade via the Erie Canal, and more people flooded into Buffalo than ever before.

During Reconstruction and throughout the rest of the 1800s, Buffalo, like many other cities in the nation, was highly impacted by the iron and steel industry. The steel industry became a formidable one during these years largely due to the evolution of the railways and the patriotic feeling of Manifest Destiny. After the Civil War, Buffalo served as a port for the country's western expansionism.

Although a center of commerce, Western New York would not become a main industrial hub until the turn of the century. The iron and steel industry helped build Buffalo into the iconic Progressive Era city embodied by the Pan-American Exposition of 1901. Steel coffers also contributed to making Buffalo a millionaires' capital, boasting more millionaires than any other city in the nation. Many of these industrial leaders built their Gilded Age palaces along the tree-lined parkways and avenues that meandered through the city.

By 1900, the metalliferous industries had firmly settled into the region. That year, ground was broken at Stony Point, an area just southwest of Buffalo in what was then the town of West Seneca. This land was purchased by local industrialist John J. Albright and his company, the Stony Point Land Company. It was then sold to the Lackawanna Iron & Steel Company of Scranton, Pennsylvania. Started originally in 1840, the Scranton & Platt Company manufactured one of the first rail mills in the country. In 1853, Scranton & Platt became the Lackawanna Iron & Coal Company. In 1891, Lackawanna merged with the Scranton Steel Company, becoming the Lackawanna Iron & Steel Company.

By 1899, it had become evident that a change in location would be to the company's advantage. Lackawanna's first choice was Lebanon, Pennsylvania, where the company had already acquired interest in blast furnaces and ore mines. Further study of the area proved the railway facility and water supply to be inadequate, however, and the Lebanon plan was quickly abandoned. Officials arrived in Buffalo to review a new location.

Western New York boasted a strong and growing workforce and an evolving consumer market. Most importantly, Buffalo had become a major railway hub and there was water in abundance from Lake Erie and Niagara Falls. Buffalo had quickly become a leading American city, and plans were already being drawn up for the 1901 Pan-American Exposition that would be hosted here. While John J. Albright sat on the board for the Pan-American Exposition committee, he was also buying up the Stony Point property. The public hypothesized that this empty land south of the city line was to be the site of the Pan-American Exposition. They could not have been more wrong.

A meeting took place at the city's prominent Buffalo Club between Lackawanna officials and leading financiers, industrialists, and politicians. It was then announced that the Lackawanna

Iron & Steel Company would be relocated to Buffalo. The new Lackawanna Steel Company would be the largest steel manufacturer in the world. The company was reorganized in 1902 in order to finance the adventure, and new board members were added, including Cornelius Vanderbilt, Walter Scranton, Moses Taylor, K.S. Van Cortland, Samuel Mather, J.G. McCullough, and other prominent men. The plant began operations in 1903.

Lackawanna was not the only steel company in town. The Tonawanda Iron Works had been operating in North Tonawanda since 1890. The Buffalo & Susquehanna Iron Company was also organized in 1900. In 1906, the Wickwire Steel Company and the Seneca Iron & Steel Company were established. The Atlas Crucible Steel Company was established in Dunkirk. In 1908, Cleveland-based firm M.A. Hanna & Company set plans in motion to build a $3 million plant in the area. The Ryerson Steel Company purchased Lancaster Steel in 1914. The New York State Steel Company, which had been in operation since 1905, became the Donner Steel Company in 1916. These, plus a number of other smaller outfits, iron companies, steel forges, manufacturing companies, and other mills made Western New York a steelworkers' paradise.

Iron and steel were not the only materials being made in Western New York's quickly growing metalliferous industries. Between 1906 and 1914, more than 750,000 pounds of copper and brass was being manufactured locally. A number of rolling mills were also producing bronze and aluminum throughout the region, and Buffalo had already been known as the grain capital of the world. Breweries, farm equipment manufacturers, elevator companies, and iron furnaces gave way to large producers of steel and steel products. European immigrants and African American migrants poured into the region seeking employment at the mills. Western New York's rich cultural heritage and diversity comes from the workers who came here looking for jobs.

By the onset of World War I, Buffalo was producing millions of tons of steel per year. By 1920, many of the mills were operating at full capacity, and the industry was already employing more than 25 percent of the local population. These numbers would triple by the end of World War II. In the 1940s, more women and minorities entered the industry's workforce than ever before because of massive wartime labor shortages and high demand. Defense plants were producing record amounts of steel and other manufactured products.

The postwar years brought unequalled prosperity to the industry and to the rest of Western New York. This was short-lived; by the 1960s, the atmosphere was beginning to change. The steel and automobile industries, the strong backbone of Western New York's manufacturing economy, began to fall apart. Failure to modernize local plants or build new plants and equipment contributed to the rise of local companies' deficits. Coupled with enormous worker salaries and pension benefits, American-made steel prices remained high. Steel was being manufactured more cheaply overseas, and steel imports were on the rise. The steel industry had plateaued, and by the end of the 1970s, plants began laying off workers and closing plants throughout the region.

In the early 1980s, Pres. Ronald Reagan was advised to establish import quotas. The president refused the relief plan, instead negotiating voluntary restraint arrangements. Congress followed by passing legislation giving the office of the president the authority to enforce the restraint arrangements. This was done on the condition that United States steel manufacturers would update their plants and equipment as well as offer training assistance to workers who had been laid off. Unfortunately, this statute was not completely followed.

In 1984, the United Steelworkers of America filed a petition with the Bethlehem Steel Company, under the Trade Act of 1974, seeking relief from imported steel products. Foreign steel producers warned that if the petition was filed, the restraint arrangements would be void. The US Trade Commission deliberated and reached a verdict, concluding that the American steel industry was indeed injured by the onslaught of foreign steel imports. Although foreign exporters seemed to cooperate with the restraint arrangements, import levels remained high, declining only slightly in each year of the program. In 1987, imports from countries without out such agreements rose sharply, and would continue to rise.

The union had originally agreed to file the joint petition with Bethlehem Steel on the grounds that new furnaces would be built and updates would be made to the plants still operating under the Bethlehem Steel sign. This would not come to fruition. Most of the steel plants across the country had already been downsized by about 70 percent, and the industry would not recover. Most of the major American steel manufacturing companies, including those in Western New York, had filed for bankruptcy by the early 2000s.

Pain was added to suffering when former steelworkers began to experience symptoms of various cancers, mesothelioma, and other diseases brought on by their experiences working in the local steel industry. Ed and Joyce Walker, along with many other former Western New York steelworkers, worked effortlessly to introduce reform into the compensation programs that offered support for workers who experienced radiation-related health complications. Mr. Walker, and so many other workers, suffered cancers and other illnesses as a result of exposure while working at the Lackawanna plant during Bethlehem Steel's Cold War nuclear program. Former steelworkers who are ill, and bereaved loved ones who remain, are still fighting to lay claim to compensation that can help provide much-needed funding for medical bills and debt.

Today, Buffalo's population is less than it was during the Pan-American Exposition of 1901. Western New York, like so many other areas around the Great Lakes, became part of the large Rust Belt. The steel industry took off and led the region into unprecedented economic heights. Then, the region began the downward spiral of financial despair, a decline that would be forever echoed across the plains and valleys of Western New York.

One

LOCATION, LOCATION, LOCATION

Eugene Grace, the president of Bethlehem Steel Company, once said, "You have the best location in the country for the successful assembly, production, and distribution of manufactured goods. There is none better, more strategically located center than Buffalo."

In the 1840s, there were only a handful of foundries and machine shops throughout Western New York. This cottage-based industry produced basic iron amenities, including agricultural tools, stoves, nails, and the like. Iron slowly found its way to Buffalo via the Erie Canal. Rail lines were not installed throughout the region until the 1850s. The railway ushered in an era of iron manufacturing, and, by the 1860s, Buffalo held a monopoly in iron-made goods. Buffalo Iron & Nail Works produced more than 15,000 pounds of nails per day, making them the largest iron producer in the region.

In 1899, it was announced that the Lackawanna Iron & Steel Company would relocate to the Buffalo area, ushering in a new age of manufacturing to Western New York. The Progressive Era brought a great many changes to the region and jumpstarted the local economy.

Lackawanna and other steel companies moved their operations to the area in order to take advantage of its central location. The region offered ease of shipping via the Great Lakes and the railroad. Raw materials and finished products could be easily shipped to and from Western New York. The area was quickly growing, and labor was easy to find, as new populations of immigrants poured into the city in search of work. Buffalo became the Queen City of the Lakes because of its growing wealth, beauty, and influence.

This postcard of the Main Office Building in Lackawanna dates from about 1912. The building is shown in all its grandeur, after the south annex was completed to make room for needed administrative space. Electrical power was also being used, as evidenced by the electric pole and wires. The automobile in front reflects a new century focused on technological advancement and huge economical change for Western New York.

This photograph shows early construction at Stony Point, in 1900, at what was to become the Lackawanna Steel Company. On October 20, 1903, the first blow from the Bessemer converter No. 1 marked the beginning of steelmaking at the Lackawanna plant. Stony Point was an area just south of Buffalo in what was then the town of West Seneca.

Laborers are seen here working on the rail mill No. 1 foundations at the Lackawanna plant in early 1900. Most of these mills were not in full operation until 1903 or 1904. Seven rolling mills were in operation by 1906. Lackawanna manufactured a number of finished products, including railing for railroads. Rolling mills were responsible for producing final steel products.

Even the hardest of winters could not deter construction at the new Lackawanna plant. Workers are seen here amidst the snow in front of the skeleton of one new building nearing completion and the foundation of another building just started. Lackawanna would be called the largest steel plant in the world.

The huge foundations of blooming mill No. 7 are seen here during construction. This early photograph shows the buildings already constructed in the background. A man stands in the upper left looking across the foundations, bringing into perspective their actual size and the size of the building that would sit on top of them.

This photograph from the early days of the Lackawanna plant shows the coke oven batteries. Coke was a high-carbon-content fuel made from coal that was used in the steelmaking process. Although coke forms naturally, most coke used in the steelmaking process is man-made. Coke ovens were used to mix and heat bituminous coal at temperatures of more than 2,000 degrees Fahrenheit. This process yielded coke, which was then used in the manufacturing of steel. Higher-quality coke meant lower coke rates, higher productivity, and lower hot metal costs. Coke was usually used in the blast furnace steelmaking process. Coke manufacturing also produced significant amounts of air pollution.

This wooden break wall was constructed in 1899 and was one of the first structures built at the new Lackawanna plant. These break walls protected the plant's coast from the battering waves of Lake Erie. Wooden break walls were replaced by metal and cement poured walls as the wood deteriorated over time.

This photograph shows workmen dredging the Union Ship Canal. The Buffalo & Susquehanna Iron Company, which later became the Hanna Furnace Company, was built along the canal. The ship canal was an important component to the prosperous steel plants south of Buffalo. The canal was completed in 1900; soon after, Buffalo & Susquehanna was in full operation.

A canal began to take form at the Lackawanna Steel Company. The ore docks, the ship canal, and the coke ovens complex are seen here in 1903. When completed, the canal was conjoined with the Union Ship Canal and ran through the plant parallel with the coastline.

Construction of the ore docks and the dock wall neared completion in 1917. With the completion of these industrial canals, ships could dock and unload the ingredients essential to the steel manufacturing process, such as iron ore, limestone, and coal. These ships could also carry finished products from the manufacturing sites across the Great Lakes region.

The Lackawanna Steel Company was quickly recognized as one of the most formidable steel plants in the world. A forest of smokestacks rose high above the newly founded city of Lackawanna. This c. 1909 image shows how a factory and the surrounding residential area sprang up in only 10 years. On the left, residential housing constructed by the Lackawanna Steel Company is visible. Officially named Ridge Road Village, it was referred to as "New Village" by its residents and by

visitors. The grassy field across the street from the Main Office Building was used for baseball games. Behind the building, the south annex can be seen jutting out of the rear of the building. By 1910, the building had already outgrown itself and the south annex was needed for more space. The Main Office Building also added a northern extension to the front and a northern annex, which mirrored the south annex.

This photograph shows the Hanna Furnace Corporation along the Union Ship Canal. Buffalo Union Steel (or Union Furnace) Company was the original manufacturer on this site. It was purchased in 1915 by the Hanna Furnace Company, a subsidiary of the M.A. Hanna Company. In 1924, M.A. Hanna transferred Hanna Furnace, along with another local subsidiary, Donner-Hanna Coke, to National Steel in exchange for stock in that company.

This photograph was taken of the Tonawanda Iron Works in the early 1900s. Located on River Road in North Tonawanda, it was founded in 1873. The company was also known as the Tonawanda Iron & Steel Corporation. A horse and buggy can be seen along the railway lines that carried engines and cars throughout the plant. (Courtesy of the Historical Society of the Tonawandas.)

This photograph shows the main entrance to the Tonawanda Iron & Steel Company in the 1950s. By 1958, the entire plant had been modernized and rebuilt as a contemporary manufacturing facility. The plant continued to operate until it was closed in 1972. It was demolished by 1974. (Courtesy of the Historical Society of the Tonawandas.)

Taken in 1937, this image shows two security guards keeping watch at the main gate of the Seneca Iron & Steel Company. The faded name of the company can be seen on one of the buildings in the background. The company was formed in 1906. Seneca was acquired by the Bethlehem Steel Company and became part of the Lackawanna plant. Some of the buildings from Seneca Iron & Steel still stand along the north side of Milestrip Road in Blasdell.

Republic Steel Corporation's Buffalo plant is seen here between the Buffalo River, South Park Avenue, and the main railway corridor in South Buffalo. Republic Steel was once the third-largest steel manufacturer in the country, just behind United States Steel and Bethlehem Steel. Republic's Buffalo plant was just one of many that the company operated across the Great Lakes. Employing several thousand workers, Republic was a heavy competitor of Bethlehem Steel.

This aerial shot shows the Republic Steel plant on the right. The Steel Plant Museum is located at the former Buffalo Color Corporation, seen in the top left hand corner of this image. The lift bridge in the background still functions on South Park Avenue. The second lift bridge, on the left, served the company's railway line.

This aerial shot of Republic Steel shows the back of the company. The massive railway lines can be seen running through the plant and merging with the main rail corridor. An ore dock can be seen along the winding Buffalo River on the left. Ships could connect to the plant via Buffalo's inner harbor.

This aerial shot of Lackawanna's coke oven batteries reflects the heavy use of the growing plant. By the 1920s, the Lackawanna Steel Company's equipment had aged and the company suffered from huge financial losses. The company, originally organized in the 1840s, could not outrun the growing corporations who were acquiring smaller companies. Eventually, a buyout was the only answer to their massive debts.

By the 1920s, the Lackawanna Steel Company had become obsolete due to lack of investments and improvements. As a result, the company began to falter and suffered from monstrous deficits. The Bethlehem Steel Company acquired Lackawanna Steel in 1922 and quickly took on the task of upgrading the plant's equipment and facilities.

Two

SHIPPING AND TRANSPORTATION

Western New York's role in the steel industry is directly linked to transportation. With its central location, Buffalo was an important port on Lake Erie and served as a gateway to the west. During the era of the Erie Canal, horses and sometimes oxen and mules pulled boats from New York City to Buffalo. Later, the steam engine increased speed and productivity and opened the door for shipping and rail to Western New York.

Buffalo was not only a destination for boats and the train; it was also home to the industries that manufactured the ships, trains, and rails themselves. The steel industry and the shipping and rail industries worked hand in hand. Transportation was fundamental to success, with the movement of coal, ore, limestone, and finished products by boat and train to and from the mills as well as throughout mill property. The South Buffalo Railway operated all standard gauge rail and locomotives used in interplant transportation. This included transportation of goods and materials to and from the ore docks as well as the removal of slag pots from the hearths to the slag drops along the coast of the plant. Republic Steel and other companies also maintained their own company-wide railways.

In total, Bethlehem Steel operated 150 locomotives, 4,000 coal cars, and 10,000-ton ore carrying vessels with a total carrying capacity of 250,000 tons per trip. If placed on a single track, the line would reach from New York City to Pittsburgh. From the Lackawanna plant, rail offered economical delivery of products to New England and the East Coast. Materials could also travel by rail or water to Detroit, Cleveland, Chicago, and other consumer cities along the Great Lakes and beyond.

Bethlehem Steel Company had a fleet of 25 ships that carried a capacity of over five million tons; seven of the larger ships could carry over 20,000 tons. Its ore came from mountain ranges throughout the Great Lakes district that was directly hauled to its docks from the Upper Lake ports.

These aerial shots of the Bethlehem Steel Company's Lackawanna plant were taken in 1928. The plant was growing, occupying space on both sides of the Hamburg Turnpike. Bethlehem Steel would eventually reach from the Union Ship Canal in the north to Woodlawn Beach in the south. Riparian rights granted to the plant by the state changed and were extended farther into Lake Erie as the company evolved. Slag and other deposits being dumped into the water along the coast built up a significant amount of man-made fill reaching deeper and deeper into the waterfront. After the transfer to the Bethlehem Steel Company in 1922, the Lackawanna plant was modernized and expanded to accommodate more advanced steel production.

The South Buffalo Railway was incorporated in 1899. This photograph shows the South Buffalo roundhouse, once located south of Ridge Road in Lackawanna. Taken in 1908, the image shows employees and the railway's prized locomotives. The railway could make connections throughout the areas south and west of Buffalo. Originally focused on the movement of passengers, the South Buffalo Railway carried an average of 600,000 people a year.

This photograph of an unidentified South Buffalo Railway worker holding an oilcan was taken in the early 1900s. Originally, the Lackawanna Steel Company operated its own railroad throughout its plant. This changed in 1903 when the South Buffalo Railway took over and managed all standard gauge tracks and locomotives at the plant.

This photograph, taken during the plant's construction, shows the Lackawanna Steel Company pay car surrounded by construction employees near the company's new coke ovens. In 1910, a new trolley line was built between Buffalo and Erie, Pennsylvania. Annual passenger capacity dwindled to 44,000. The railroad would take over exclusive operation of interplant rail transportation.

Railway lines near the blast furnace area at the Lackawanna plant can be seen in this undated photograph. Slag vessels travel behind a locomotive on the right. Rail lines were condensed throughout the plant, and sometimes at least three or four tracks would run alongside one another.

Buffalo Creek Railway's engine No. 25 is the subject of this undated photograph. The railroad was established in 1869 to serve the Lehigh Valley Railroad coal trestle. This was one of a handful of trestles to serve the massive movement of coal west from Buffalo. Buffalo Creek Railroad remained in operation until it was merged into Conrail in 1983.

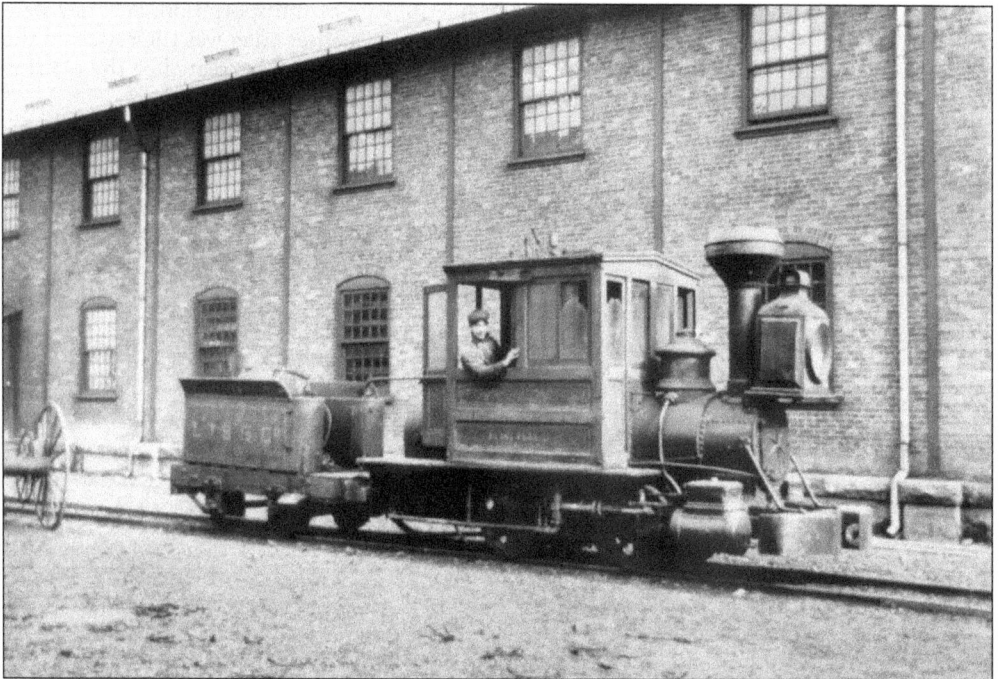

This photograph shows an early Lackawanna Steel Company locomotive on the plant. This narrow gauge locomotive was originally used at the plant in Scranton, Pennsylvania, and was moved to the new plant in West Seneca. Its purpose was to shift small cars between various buildings on the plant's grounds. Steelmaking materials and finished products were moved throughout the plant in this manner. (Courtesy of the Western New York Railway Historical Society, collection of Paul Pietrak.)

This photograph shows an early steel mill employee dumping slag into Lake Erie. The lakes and tributaries throughout the region allowed wonderful ease of transportation, but they were also highly polluted as a result of their overuse as a waste dispenser. Slag was the runoff of the steelmaking process. In Lackawanna, windmills stand on land that was created by the pouring of slag on the lake side of the former plant.

This 1950 photograph shows a string of ladle cars, which were used to dump slag along the Lake Erie shoreline, brought to a halt by a derailed locomotive. Behind the locomotive is a power car that provided the air pressure to tilt the ladles so they could dump their molten contents. (Courtesy of the Western New York Railway Historical Society.)

This photograph shows workers posed with a narrow gauge locomotive. *Narrow gauge* simply refers to the distance between the rails of a railway. Narrow gauges are smaller than a standard gauge line, and benefit industries and smaller communities. Also primarily developed as an industrial railroad, narrow gauge lines are still in use in factories, towns, and cities for the movement of both goods and people.

South Buffalo Railway locomotive No. 7 is seen in this early photograph. The 2-8-0 locomotive was built new for the South Buffalo Railway in 1903. This builder's photograph from the Baldwin Locomotive Works shows it in pinstriping and with painted wheels. This locomotive likely started as a passenger service, hauling steelworkers from Buffalo out to the steel plant. (Courtesy of Ronald R. Dukarm.)

These two photographs show South Buffalo Railway engines No. 16 and No. 85. Both images were taken at the Lackawanna plant. The advancements made in the railway throughout the 1900s are evident in the comparison of these two images. The later engines, like No. 85, were yellow and black and were iconic images of the South Buffalo Railway. For more than 100 years, the South Buffalo Railway transported passengers and goods through South Buffalo and the Lackawanna plant. As the Bethlehem Steel Company shut down operations in Lackawanna between 1983 and 2001, South Buffalo Railways was rendered useless and remained in the company's possession until it was sold to Genesee & Wyoming Inc.

Taken in the 1950s, this photograph shows the South Buffalo Railway overpass above Route 5, looking south toward Hamburg. The Lackawanna plant had grown so much that operations were built on both sides of Route 5. This was a major connection between the east and west plant properties. (Courtesy of the Western New York Railway Historical Society.)

This 1977 photograph shows the *Belle River* afloat on Lake Erie. This was one of dozens of ships that transported raw materials and finished products to and from the industries that dotted the Western New York coastline. Ships like this one would make connections throughout the Great Lakes region.

This photograph from the early 1900s shows the dredging of the ship canal. Ore-handling equipment and parts of Lackawanna's blast furnaces can be seen in the background. Rail tracks can also be seen on the right. When completed, ships would dock and deliver ore and other products needed to make steel at the local plants.

Taken in 1907, this image from a postcard shows the Tonawanda Iron & Steel Company's plant in North Tonawanda. The postcard reports, "The Twin Cities are growing on account of their unequalled Advantages to Manufacturers." The company was strategically located on the Niagara River just between Lake Erie and Ontario, Canada.

Shipping was important to the manufacturing of steel in Western New York. This photograph shows the west side of the Union Ship Canal and another view of Hanna Furnace. A worker is on the dock just beyond the first ship in the foreground, showing the enormity of the operation. The mouth to Lake Erie can be seen faintly in the distance.

This 1953 photograph shows the Lackawanna plant's ore storage yard, with a self-unloading boat unloading dolomite into hopper No. 1's massive conveyor belt. Mastering the Great Lakes, companies like Bethlehem could transport ore and other materials quickly and cheaply by the mid-1900s.

Upkeep of the canals meant that new base walls were repaired and restored while older, more used ones were replaced. Taken in 1953, this photograph shows the new wall on the ore dock's south side of the ship canal, looking southeast at Bethlehem's Lackawanna plant.

Another 1953 shot of Lackawanna's ore docks, this photograph shows the ore dock anchorage just north of the transfer table. The Hulett transfer table, as it was called, moved the ships away from the dock to allow ore bridge cranes, like the ones seen on the right, to pass by.

This 1961 photograph looks northeast, showing blast furnace No. 8's ore bridge at Bethlehem Steel's Lackawanna plant. From delivery of the iron ore to the wrapping of the finished steel product, the manufacturing of steel was an intricate process. The unloading of iron ore was made to be more efficient as time progressed.

These two photographs show the unloading of ore vessels at Bethlehem Steel's Lackawanna plant. The Hulett Iron Ore Unloader was invented in 1908. First powered by steam and then by electricity, the Hulett Unloader was fitted with a grab bucket that was used to unload iron ore from the belly of ore-carrying ships throughout the Great Lakes. These unloaders, operated first with a 10-ton bucket and then with a 17-ton bucket, were able to unload 1,000 tons per hour each. More than one unloader was used on each ore ship, making the unloading processes faster and easier.

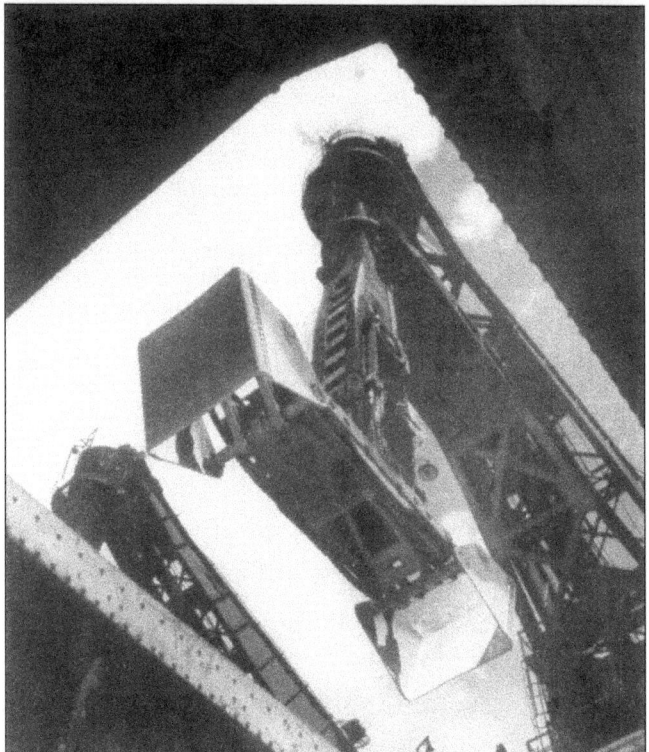

Taken on May 10, 1960, during a director's tour of Bethlehem Steel Company's Lackawanna plant, this photograph shows the stern of the *Arthur B. Homer*. Company directors are standing behind the railing. Built at Great Lakes Engineering Works in River Rouge, Michigan, the *Arthur B. Homer* sailed the lengths of the Great Lakes and was in use, mainly by the Lackawanna plant, until 1980. When Bethlehem started closing its plants in the late 1970s and early 1980s, the shipping fleets, like the railways, became expendable. The *Homer* was not a self-unloader, so it was deemed obsolete. It was laid up in Erie, Pennsylvania, along with another great Bethlehem ore ship, the *Johnson*, until it was eventually sold for scrap. The *Homer* was towed to Ontario and then dismantled, while the *Johnson* met a similar fate after being towed to Spain.

Three

MADE IN THE USA

The evolution of steelmaking offered a growth in productivity in Western New York. Blast furnaces, open-hearth furnaces, and basic oxygen furnaces helped increase steelmaking across the region. Effective technological achievements helped increase product quality and quantity. During the two world wars, productivity increased due to supply meeting wartime demands.

As World War II came to an end, the production of defense materials came to a halt. The Cold War years brought suburban sprawl to Western New York. As the region returned to a sense of normality, the steel industry slowly settled into a routine of consumer supply and demand. Many women returned to the home but some remained in the workplace. More women and minorities held positions in the steel industry than ever before, and that was not about to change. In many cases, there were fewer jobs to be had when veterans returned home.

Postwar prosperity led to a lull in production. However, the steel industry became the epitome of the American dream: a home in the suburbs, a steelworker, his stay-at-home wife, a son, a daughter, a dog, and an American-made car. This was a typical life for many families throughout Western New York. As wars, politics, and unionization collided in the first half of the 1900s, the steel industry supported much of Western New York's working class. This generation of steelworkers provided for the opportunities of their descendants. The children of the industrial class were able to attend college and secure careers outside the fire and brimstone of the steel industry. Second- and third-generation steelworkers were beginning to enter the middle class.

By 1955, Buffalo's steel and automobile industry boasted more than 60,000 employees. Bethlehem Steel Corporation had been inflated by huge war profits and began to buy up smaller companies throughout the nation. Three generations of American families had poured steel in Western New York since 1900. By the 1960s, Bethlehem Steel expanded their annual capacity to more than 5.7 million tons. Bethlehem's Lackawanna plant had become the third-largest steel producer in the world, with a workforce of more than 21,000 men and women, supported by a payroll of almost $120 million. These were the peak years for Western New York's steel industry.

Taken in 1933, this photograph shows the motor generators sitting at a powerhouse at a local steel plant. Originally steamed by coal, power was harnessed using large tonnages of coal. However, the close location of Niagara Falls helped improve this situation even more. Hydroelectric power from the falls was much cheaper, cleaner, and more efficient. Local steel plants were quick to change to electric.

This photograph shows the blast furnaces at Bethlehem Steel's Lackawanna plant. Blast furnaces were used in the smelting of iron. Fuel (coke), iron ore, and flux (limestone) were poured through the top of the furnace, while air was blown into the lower part of the furnace. Molten iron and slag were tapped at the bottom of the furnace while gasses were emitted from the top.

These photographs show the repairs of the foundations of blast furnace G at the Lackawanna plant in 1962 and 1963. The images show the erection of steelwork for the furnace and the cast house. The cast house is the bottom portion of the blast furnace. Here, the molten iron and slag, once tapped, would flow down a shallow trench, or runner, in the cast house floor, which would separate into multiple tributaries where they would spill into ladles below the edge of the floor. Molten iron would either be cast in ingots along the runner (pig iron) or go on to the next stage of molten iron. These ladles were then used to separate and relocate the molten iron and slag. The tapholes were then plugged by refractory clay. Blast furnaces would run continuously, with the exception of occasional planned repairs and maintenance.

These images show the newly constructed blast furnace J at Bethlehem Steel Company's Lackawanna plant in 1952. Bethlehem continued to expand operations, including the building of new furnaces like blast furnace J, during its years of postwar prosperity. Below, a worker can be seen at the casting floor lifting a dam in the runner at the base of the blast furnace, allowing a river of molten iron and slag to flow freely downstream toward the ladles. Boots, a thick coat, gloves, safety glasses, and a helmet protect the worker from the heat and potential splash of molten pig iron. Some furnaces had more than one taphole and included a skimmer used to separate the slag from the liquid iron, as well as more than one cast house.

This photograph, taken during Bethlehem's foundation repairs of blast furnace G in 1963, looks northwest along the east side of the cast house while the furnace is in operation. Vessels sit atop a narrow gauge rail track. These vessels would be filled with slag, as seen, below the blast furnace's cast house floor. Slag pots would be taken to the coast of the Lackawanna plant and dumped into the water. Today, a series of windmills stand on land created by these slag heaps. The iron was intended for refining in the next stage of steelmaking, usually at the open-hearth or basic oxygen furnaces.

This photograph shows the first step of open-hearth furnace production. Taken around 1950, it shows a furnace being charged with molten iron, adding to the scrap and flux in the furnace. Making steel was like preparing a stew in a pot: specific ingredients were needed to create the perfect final product.

A furnace in No. 1 open-hearth shop is seen here tapping steel into ladle No. 6. This 1956 photograph shows the process where molten steel is tapped and flows into a ladle. Once filled, slag would form on the top and flow off the sides of the ladle. The open-hearth was one of many kinds of furnaces where excess carbon and impurities were burnt out of molten iron to produce steel.

This photograph shows a double furnace tapping at the No. 2 open-hearth at Bethlehem's Lackawanna plant. The plant did not use these double furnaces after 1967. Slag can be seen running off the sides of these ladles, while a hook waits to move the vessels to the next step of steelmaking.

This photograph offers another view of tapping an open-hearth furnace. The molten steel is flowing into a ladle, and slag can be seen running from the top into a slag vessel off to the side. The slag ladles would be removed and dumped while the ladle of molten steel was used in the next steelmaking process.

The image below shows a frontal view of open-hearth slag runoff and slag pot stands. The vessel containing the molten steel has already been removed, while the slag ladle on the left is full, waiting to be removed and dumped at the slag heaps.

The Lackawanna plant's open-hearth shops, seen here in 1958, would cast raw steel into ingot molds in a process known as teeming. After tapping an open-hearth, the ladle of molten steel would be picked up and moved over ingot molds. This ladle would then be opened and molten steel would pour out into the molds. The photograph below shows the pouring of leaded steel heat in No. 2 open-hearth.

This photograph shows a foreman directing a charging crane operator to pour molten iron into the basic oxygen furnace. In the 1850s, Henry Bessemer invented the process of blowing air into molten iron to reduce carbon content, thus producing a low-carbon steel. The process was refined by Robert Durrer in the 1940s by replacing air with oxygen, making the process faster and cheaper.

This photograph shows the process of charging molten iron from the blast furnace into the basic oxygen furnace vessel to be converted into steel. It is called *basic* because of the calcium and magnesium oxide refractory bricks that line the furnace, which are capable of withstanding the high temperatures of molten iron. Pig iron and scrap metal were charged into a basic oxygen furnace.

These photographs of Bethlehem Steel Company's Lackawanna plant show two more views of the process known as charging the basic oxygen furnace. Once a furnace was charged, the vessel would be tilted upright and oxygen would be blown into the mixture, melting the scrap and igniting the carbon in the iron, releasing as carbon monoxide and dioxide. Fluxes like limestone or dolomite are added to the ingredients to form slag, which then catches the impurities that are removed in the tapping process. The vessel is tilted again and molten steel is then tapped into a ladle. Oxygen is used instead of air, as in the Bessemer process, because it is far more efficient in the smelting process.

These photographs, taken at Bethlehem Steel in the 1960s, show the advancements of the basic oxygen furnace. Above, a ladle charges the vessel. Then, the vessel is tilted upright, and oxygen is blown in, and flux is added during the blowing step. The oxygen creates a mixture that is hotter than 3,000 degrees Fahrenheit. In all of these processes, the main purpose is to take iron and create steel by lowering the carbon and impurity contents. The more carbon in the product, the harder and more brittle it will be. The lower the carbon, the stronger and more flexible it will be. Slag, the main by-product of the steelmaking process, is the mixture of carbon and impurities pulled out of the molten steel mixture. The photograph below shows the tapping of a basic oxygen furnace vessel.

This photograph shows the process of teeming a leaded heat in the basic oxygen furnace. Here, workers are shooting a stream of lead into the molten steel. This photograph was taken at the No. 1 pouring platform at Bethlehem Steel's Lackawanna plant. The hoods were used to draw off lead fumes while the lead was injected into the stream of molten steel. The addition of lead added machinability to some steel grades.

Taken on October 31, 1968, this photograph shows a railcar dumping slag into Lake Erie at Bethlehem Steel's Lackawanna plant. This location was the No. 10 drop. As more and more steel was produced, the by-product slag was also being produced with incalculable speed. Throughout the 80 years that the Lackawanna plant was manufacturing, the amounts of slag that accumulated along its coast continuously added man-made land to the site. As a result, riparian grants given by the state had to be increased throughout the life of the plant.

This photograph shows an ingot being placed in a soaking pit at the 45-by-90 slab mill at the Bethlehem Steel Company's Lackawanna plant. These refractory lined pits "soaked" the cold ingots in heat until they were hot enough throughout to be rolled into slabs. The slabs then headed to the hot strip mill for further processing.

This 1965 photograph shows the slurrying of a mold at the No. 4 mold yard. Slurrying a mold involved coating the inside of the mold to prevent the ingot from sticking to the mold. Ingots usually separated from the molds due to expansion and contraction during the cooling process. The coating also prevented slag from sticking to the cast-iron slag pots.

Bethlehem Steel's galvanizing plant is seen here. The photograph was taken looking east at the delivery section from the flux-drying tower in Lackawanna. The galvanized mill produced coated sheet steel for a number of different products. Coils of steel from the cold mill were delivered to the galvanized mill to be cleaned, trimmed, and coated to meet customer specifications.

Lackawanna's hot strip mill is seen here. The hot strip mill would take blooms, slabs, or billets and convert them into sheet steel or simple cross-sectional steel products. Sheet steel was high in demand by the automobile industry. Sheet steel was and is used for the production of car bodies and other products, including household appliances.

Four

LIFE INSIDE THE PLANT

The steel plants in Western New York functioned as small cities. Some employed hundreds of workers, while others, like Bethlehem Steel's Lackawanna plant, employed 20,000. These plants usually ran 24 hours a day. Individual departments were responsible for running affectively and efficiently. Stopping for costly repairs and harmful accidents would cost the companies' time, money, and workers. Safety was the main concern for workers in the plants. Fire and injury were common due to the size and magnitude of the machinery used to produce steel. The plant was a very dangerous environment, especially for those who were careless and did not work with caution.

Steel plants relied on not just the steelworkers to accomplish their goals, but also on administrators, fire and security departments, engineers, metallurgists, and transportation employees to do their part and ensure the plant ran smoothly and without incident. When accidents and repairs did occur, these workers were expected to be responsive and responsible. Life in the plant was the daily reality for hundreds of thousands of Western New Yorkers. It was not always easy, and it was not taken lightly. The steel companies throughout the region had high expectations of their workers. To let down the company could mean automatic dismissal.

The working class quickly evolved into the middle class. Second- and third-generation steelworkers were often the products of the homes of first-generation Americans, and working in the steel plants was often a family affair. It was important that employees knew about and looked out for their coworkers. No worker could know everyone at the company, but it was important for employees to know their mill and understand how it operated.

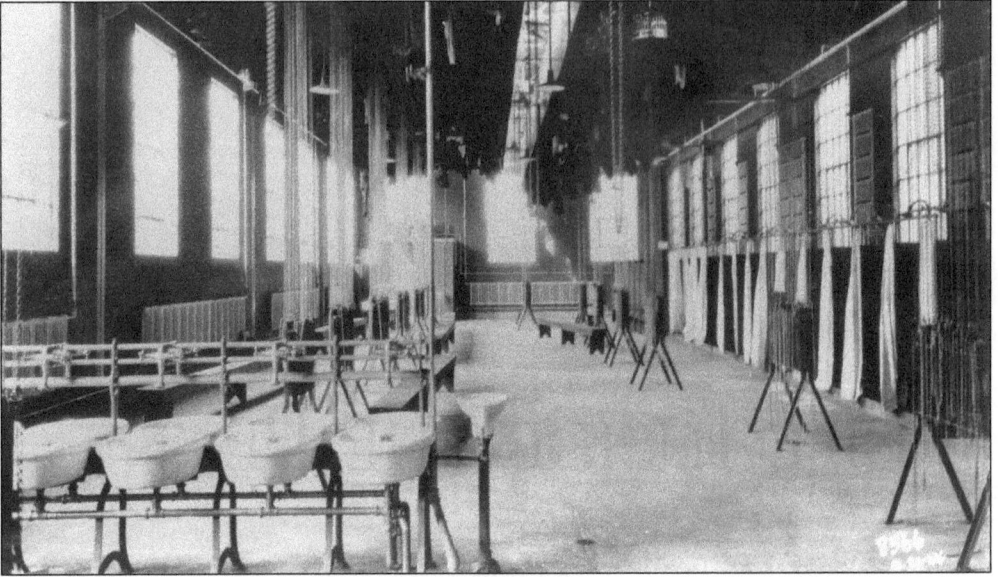

Each division in the plant had its own welfare buildings. Due to the large population of the workforce, simple locker rooms would not suffice. These buildings, like this blast furnace welfare building, included restroom facilities, showers, and baskets in which workers would store their belongings. The baskets would then be hoisted to the ceiling to save space and protect their contents.

The welfare building for open-hearth No. 1 in Lackawanna is seen here on Christmas Eve 1940. With the room decorated for the holidays, men sit at rest on the benches. Their belongings hang from the ceiling, suspended in baskets. The ornaments on the tree include messages such as "Sound Limbs," "Family Security," and "Fingers."

This photograph was taken in 1934 of Bethlehem Steel's roll shop employees at the Lackawanna plant. On the right, a sign reads, "654 days with no accidents." These signs were scattered throughout the mills, not just in Western New York's steel plants, but in other manufacturing plants as well. Safety always played a major part in the daily lives of steelworkers.

WORLD'S RECORD BROKEN
BY C.W. CASH & CREW ON
THE 76" TANDEM MILL
– MAY-29-1939 –
1,349,049 #
BETH. STL. CO.- LACKA. PLT.

15170
7-13-39

Taken on July 13, 1939, this photograph shows Bethlehem Steel employees posed at the Lackawanna plant's tandem mill. The photograph reads, "World's Record Broken by C.W. Cash and Crew on the 76" Tandem Mill, May 29, 1939; 1,349, 049 pounds; Bethlehem Steel's Lackawanna Plant." The region's steel production would increase even more over the next 20 years.

This photograph, probably taken in the early 1930s, shows a large group of steelworkers. Some men are in work clothes and coveralls, while others wear ties and dress coats. They pose in front of one of the many buildings at the Lackawanna plant. Rail lines run in front of them, and large ducts run across the face of the building behind them.

Workers pose for a photograph at one of the region's many plants. This photograph, taken in the years leading up to World War II, offers an insight to the camaraderie of steelworkers on the job. Helmets had not yet been enforced at the Bethlehem plant.

This photograph shows a group of workers in the process of changing a valve. Goggles can be seen on some of the workers' heads, and they are all wearing thick protective clothing, including coveralls, gloves, and hats, although helmets are still not worn yet. These men probably worked in a blast furnace at Bethlehem Steel's Lackawanna plant before the outbreak of World War II.

African American workers pose at blast furnace J at the Lackawanna plant in 1952. A rapid stream of African American workers moved north during the Great Migration, seeking jobs in Detroit, Pittsburgh, Chicago, and Buffalo. US Census records report that only 32 African Americans lived in Buffalo in 1820. By 1900, there were more than 1,600. By 1960, more than 70,000 African Americans called Buffalo home.

Two unidentified Bethlehem Steel employees stand next to the ship canal at the Lackawanna plant in 1953. By the 1950s, Bethlehem was booming. The plant produced rails, tie plates, spikes, bars, slabs, sheet metal, billets, structural shapes, sheet piling, and structural steel fabrications. The Lackawanna plant employed more than 20,000 men and women and boasted to be the world's largest steel plant.

The 1960s photograph below shows an unidentified worker maneuvering his way through the plant during a shift change. This scene would repeat itself a number of times per day for a great many workers in numerous plants across Western New York. The plants operated day and night for seven days a week and 365 days a year.

Two workers clean ingot molds in a basic oxygen furnace shop. Workmen would be swung over the molds on a lift where they could see down into the mold in order to clean out remnants from the teeming process. The molds could be reused a number of times before needing repair or replacement.

This photograph of steelworkers was taken in 1967. By the 1960s, steel imports to the United States were on the upswing. Huge employment wages and salaries coupled with massive benefits and pensions left domestic steel manufacturing costs high. There was also a lull in steel demand, and domestic steel companies began to lose out on customers and contracts.

Like so many other manufacturers in the region, the Republic Steel Company owned and maintained its own railway for interplant transportation. These photographs show workers at Republic Steel's locomotive and car repair shop around 1970. The steel industry not only included steelworkers, but also rail men, nurses, administrative personnel, engineers, scientists, cafeteria workers, and more. The devastation that came in the wake of the region's plant closings not only affected union and salaried employees, but also the many men and women who relied on the local companies for income, insurance, and pensions. When basic steel manufacturing was shut down, so were the many other departments that relied on it.

The photograph above, from the 1970s, shows a worker and a coiling mandrel. Sheet steel became a major product for Bethlehem Steel, a company proud of their product quality. Here, a metallurgical inspector watches sheet steel as it coils, looking for any imperfections, or "bubbles," in the steel.

This photograph shows sheet steel exiting a zinc bath at Bethlehem's galvanized division in Lackawanna. The molten zinc bath coated the sheet steel, preventing corrosion, as zinc is more resistant to corrosion than steel. This was done after the sheet steel was annealed, rolled to customers' specifications, and cleaned.

After sheet steel was produced by a rolling mill, it was stored before it went on to the next step in the process, usually to the galvanized products division. This photograph shows the coil storage area in one of the rolling mills at Bethlehem Steel Company's Lackawanna plant.

Taken in 1958, this photograph shows I-beams at the 48-inch gauge press. Workers are handling these beams at the west assembly bed. One worker mans the controls of a crane while another directs the movement of the beam. Another worker looks on, and another in the background does a final inventory and inspection of the product.

Photography was not common inside the plant. Candid shots like these, taken of Bethlehem employees in the 1970s, are hard to find. Usually, the company commissioned a photographer to take shots throughout the plant. Workers were not allowed to take photographs inside the plant itself. Bethlehem steel indexed and identified each image with a call number on the bottom of the photograph. By the 1970s, the local steel companies had begun to falter. Finally, in 1975, the world steel market crashed. A new age of foreign steel imports was dawning. In 1973, American consumption of foreign steel had risen to over 18 percent. By 1977, layoffs and plant closings were imminent.

These two photographs of workers were taken in the 1970s at retirement parties given by coworkers inside Lackawanna's basic oxygen plant. By 2003, Bethlehem Steel Company was bankrupt and sold. Bankruptcy allowed the company to lose its massive pension plan. Bethlehem Steel was sold to the International Steel Group (ISG). This company was able to persuade the union to give up the lifetime health benefits of over 95,000 retired steelworkers. Aging men and women who spent most of their lives working in the steel mills suddenly had no pension and no health benefits. ISG acquired Bethlehem Steel assets in federal bankruptcy court. Mittal Steel took over ISG in 2005 and became ArcelorMittal Steel in 2007.

Five

A COMMUNITY OF STEEL

In 2011, the Steel Plant Museum of Western New York and the Burchfield Penney Art Center (BPAC) teamed up to design an exhibit focused on the society that revolved around the local steel industry. Alana Ryder, the curator for public and academic programs at BPAC, coined the exhibit *A Community of Steel*. Many of the images in this chapter were used in the exhibit. These images identify the role that the steel industry played in the development of the region.

All areas of life were influenced by the steel industry. In 1900, the Lackawanna Steel Company built its new plant south of Buffalo. It was technically in the town of West Seneca. By 1909, the area surrounding the plant had become a small village and was established as the city of Lackawanna. Workmen housing, gardens, hospitals, and fire and police departments were all established by the steel plant.

Foreign laborers flocked to the region looking for work, mainly western and eastern European immigrants, and African Americans migrated northward. Much of the region's ethnic diversity is a result of steelworkers and their families, who relocated to the region. In 1910, more than 10,000 people worked in over 150 steel factories in Buffalo. More than half of this group was employed at Lackawanna. Another 3,600 worked in the growing automobile industry, 3,400 worked in the railway production industry, and almost 2,000 worked in the local brass and copper industries.

By the 1920s, more than 100,000 men and women were employed by local manufacturers. The United Steelworkers of America was born with the Steel Workers Organizing Committee in the 1930s. Never before had politics and religion combined in such a pivotal way, spawning a paradigm shift that would forever alter the region.

Many people raised in Western New York have close ties with someone who once was or still is employed by the steel industry. Whether it was Republic Steel, the coke producer Donner-Hanna, or the pig iron producer Hanna Furnace Corporation in Buffalo, Bethlehem Steel in Lackawanna, Wickwire-Spencer in Tonawanda, Allegheny-Ludlum in Dunkirk, Symington Gould in Depew, or Dresser-Rand in Olean, descendants of steelworkers cover the region.

The Lackawanna Steel Company built a number of housing units throughout what was then West Seneca to accommodate the growing families that came to the area seeking employment. The first of the company's housing projects was Smokes Creek Village. Referred to as the "Old Village," Smokes Creek Village is seen here around 1920. Eventually, Bethlehem Park was built by Bethlehem Steel, replacing the Old Village.

This photograph of Lackawanna's Ridge Road Village was taken in 1941. These residential homes lined Fifth Street in Lackawanna. This photograph looks east from the Hamburg Turnpike. This was the second housing unit constructed by the Lackawanna Steel Company.

Ridge Road Village, also known as New Village, incorporated row housing with single-family and two-family units, as well as large apartment-style buildings. This photograph shows homes built at the intersection of Fifth Street and Route 5 in Lackawanna. The corner property was deeded to the US government and served as the residence of the South Channel Lighthouse keeper.

This photograph from around 1950 shows more company housing in Ridge Road Village, or New Village. By the 1920s, the Lackawanna Steel Company had become the fourth-largest steel company in the nation. By 1925, Bethlehem Steel Company had become the second-largest steel producer in the world. Company housing was essential to growth at the Lackawanna plant and the community surrounding it.

These c. 1930 photographs show the Bethlehem Steel Company employee gardens. Today, the Gateway Building stands on the former grounds. Woodlawn Beach is next to where these gardens sat. Smokestacks can be seen in the background of the photograph below. Each worker and his family had an assigned plot where they would grow fruits and vegetables needed at their tables. Families of all backgrounds benefited from these gardens, especially during the Great Depression. A blueprint for these gardens can be found in the Steel Plant Museum's archives, each plot meticulously drawn and assigned to workers indicated by the family name in each square or plot.

This photograph, taken around 1930, shows Bethlehem employees and their families gardening in their plots at the employee gardens. Bethlehem equipment can be seen in the background. The steel companies in Lackawanna created a community from empty land. They built an industry, housing, gardens, and an entire urban landscape just south of Buffalo.

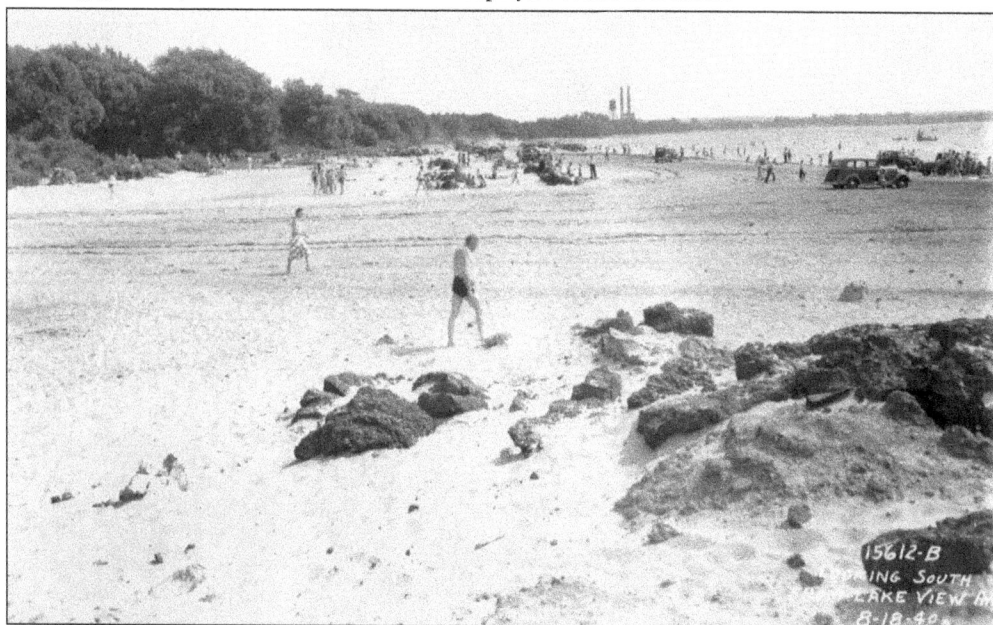

Workers and their families enjoy the beach on August 18, 1940. Originally on Bethlehem Steel property, the public beach offered a summer beach complete with an amusement park for workers and their families to enjoy during the hot summers on Lake Erie. Smokestacks from the Penn-Dixie Cement plant can be seen rising above the trees in the background.

The photograph above was taken in 1937 in front of Moses Taylor Hospital, which was built in 1903 on Ridge Road in what is now Lackawanna. Moses Taylor was a prominent industrialist and served on the Lackawanna Steel Company's board of directors. This hospital served the workers injured in the line of duty at the plant. The hospital's west ward (below) was the burn ward, and many workers were treated here for burns they incurred on the job. At the time, there were no unions and very few forms of health insurance, if any. Having a hospital close by was more than most steel plants offered their employees.

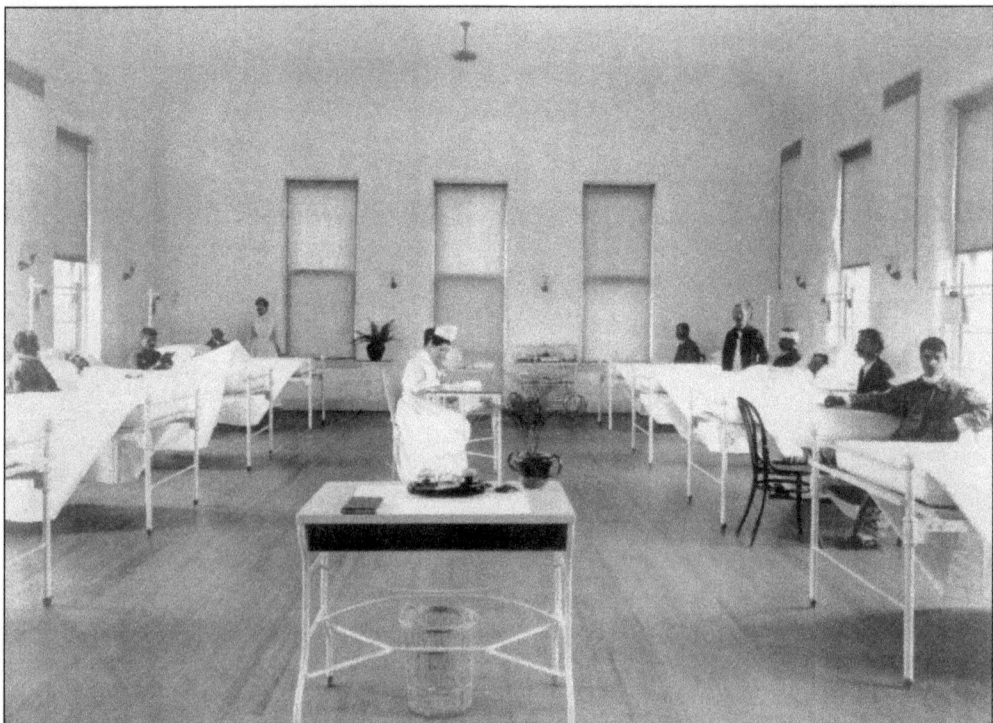

This photograph dates to the early 1900s. This early nurse tended the wounds of Lackawanna's injured workers. Women were a strong presence in the creation of the communities that sprang up around Western New York's industry. Eventually, it became more socially acceptable for women to work in the plant itself. Before and throughout the 1900s, women served as nurses, administrative assistants, cafeteria workers, and the like.

Not only was Moses Taylor Hospital constructed to serve injured workers, but a clinic was also built on Lackawanna plant property. The clinic at gate one, seen below in 1923, included ambulances and first-response tools. The clinic served injured employees and saw to their needs if they were transferred to another local hospital, like Moses Taylor, for further examination.

Outings were a popular way to socialize for many departments at the local steel mills. These 1937 photographs show the Bethlehem Steel Company's mill outing at Kudara's Grove in Hamburg (above) and the blast furnace picnic at the Hamburg Fairgrounds (below). Food, drink, and games, like the greased pole below, were provided, and steelworkers were allowed to relax and enjoy a day with their coworkers. Outings were also photographed by commissioned photographers. Both of these images show a call number in the bottom right corner. Bethlehem's managers had the Management Club in Hamburg, which is now the Briarwood Country Club. At the club, management employees were offered recreation on a regular basis. Bethlehem also had lunches and dinners at Kleinhans Music Hall in Buffalo. Republic Steel offered similar dinners at the Statler Hotel, also in Buffalo.

This 1941 photograph shows the first-annual outing of Bethlehem Steel's Lackawanna plant police department. A plant police department had been around ever since the building of the plant. Like the fire department, as the plant grew, more security was needed to patrol the plant.

This photograph shows the Bethlehem Steel Company's purchasing department outing in 1945, reflecting the administrative aspects of the steel plant. The majority of these departments were staffed by women, who held a number of positions throughout the many departments, from steelworker to purchaser.

This photograph, taken on January 15, 1956, shows the Bethlehem Steel Company's Lackawanna roll department at a luncheon meeting. The location is not disclosed, but it more than likely took place at the local union hall or at a local social club. The majority of the employees are men, but some women are seated at a table in the background.

This 1948 photograph shows the Bethlehem Steel Company's Christmas Chorus in Lackawanna. The group holds music books on their laps and at their sides. Community was important to the steel employees, especially during the holidays.

Taken in the early days of the Lackawanna Steel Company, this photograph shows steelworkers playing baseball on a field built directly across Route 5 from the plant in Lackawanna. Workers' housing is in the background. A staircase leading up to the South Buffalo Railway covered passenger platform is used as a makeshift grandstand. Steelworkers created different sports teams and a number of other amusement groups.

Bowling was a popular sport for steelworkers and their families. The No. 7 mill bowling team is seen here. More than likely taken in the 1950s, the photograph shows an advertising banner for Southside Furniture in the background. There was a fierce competition between plant departments, as well as between the different steel plants.

Buffalo and Lackawanna had innumerable pubs and bars where workers would meet for drinks. This 1950s photograph shows Bethlehem Steel employees at their favorite hangout spot. Some departments usually met at the same bar. Buffalo also had an important brewery industry as a result of the grain elevators.

Six

LABOR RELATIONS

The steel mills employed salaried employees, usually managers and other administrators, and union employees. In the 1800s, unions labor laws were nonexistent. By the early 1900s, industrial America was progressing into a labor-intensive society. As the gaps between the upper and lower classes began to grow narrower, industrialization gave way to the rising working and middle classes. Unionization would take a hold of the economic and political lives of manufacturers.

The Steel Workers Organizing Committee gave way to the United Steelworkers of America union in the late 1930s and early 1940s. Unions provided representatives, voted in by the employees they represented, to make financial and grievance agreements with the corporations. Many times, union officials and management did not get along, for obvious reasons. However, they could sometimes work together to provide concessions to better insure the workers as well as the company. By the 1980s, unions and the fading companies were at dire odds with one another.

Salaried employees received numerous benefits from the companies, while the union employees received security through wage raises and other benefits such as pensions and health insurance. Picket lines and strikes did take place in Western New York, some more infamous and violent than others. Politics, religion, and culture would collide with unions, as workers of certain creeds and backgrounds identified with specific political agendas.

These two photographs show the Lackawanna Steel Company's original police and fire departments. Both taken in 1904, the images show the two groups posed in front of the main entrance to the Main Office Building on Fuhrman Boulevard in Lackawanna. The police department stands uniformed, while the fire department stand in daily attire and overalls. Some policemen stand with the firemen, showing a link between the two departments. The firemen are posed with early fire department equipment, including two hose reels. A fire department building was constructed next to the former site of the Administration Building. The fire department remains barren and empty today.

Fire protection was one of the main areas of safety concern at any steel plant. These two photographs, taken in 1927 (above) and 1940 (below), show members of Bethlehem Steel Company's fire department. Comparing the two images, one can see the advancements made in fire equipment. Above, firemen stand in front of an early fire truck complete with ladders and a bell. The image below not only shows members of the fire department in front of a newer fire truck, but also a tanker and another truck, all boasting ladders, flood lights, and horns.

These photographs, from 1923 (above) and 1925 (below), show representatives at a fire prevention meeting. Each year, officials gathered at Bethlehem's headquarters in Bethlehem, Pennsylvania, to discuss fire prevention. Fire was a reality in many of the steel plants, as it was the basic ingredient to steel manufacturing. A number of plants suffered outbreaks of fire. Bethlehem's Lackawanna plant suffered from a number of both small and large fires throughout the 60 years it was in operation. Men were injured, equipment was damaged, and, in the case of one mill, an entire building had to be restored and put back together. Fire was on the minds of all officials at the steel plants. When damages occurred, manufacturing had to be halted and a great deal of money was lost. Injuries to workers meant not only the loss of time and money, but able, hardworking men as well.

This photograph, taken on February 13, 1961, at Bethlehem Steel's Lackawanna plant, shows an injured worker circled by his coworkers. The injured worker has bandages around is head and hand, and his arm is in a sling. Injuries occurred frequently, some more threatening than others. Hundreds of men were injured and killed every year in Western New York's steel industries.

Man on channel is in path of crane and also is in danger of roller line starting. Note condition of crane and monorail. Hand rail is broken to allow crane to pass.

This Bethlehem Steel safety inspection photograph from 1971 lists safety concerns in the bottom right corner. By the 1970s, much of the Lackawanna plant had become obsolete. The lack of investment in advancing the company technologically was one reason behind the fall of Bethlehem Steel in the 1980s. This same scenario occurred to other companies in Western New York and across the country. Failure to update and renovate the steel plants helped contribute to the downfall of America's steel industry.

Taken on Monday, August 4, 1952, this photograph shows the traffic during a morning shift change at 6:45 a.m. The Buffalo Skyway had not been built along Route 5 yet. All four lanes of traffic are congested heading in and out of the city. Cars and trucks come to a standstill to let steelworkers cross in front of Bethlehem Steel's Lackawanna plant. Workers file through the

main gate and pass through security clearance on their way into work. The Main Office Building looks on as another week begins. Since the plant ran continuously, there were no Mondays at the plant—only tomorrow and yesterday.

This photograph was taken just 15 minutes before the image on the previous page, at 6:30 a.m. on August 4, 1952. The scene would change dramatically in the next 15 minutes. These two images reflect the postwar routine that settled into 1950s Western New York.

Bethlehem Steel Company prided itself on its safety programs. This photograph from the 1960s shows a Lackawanna employee receiving a Perfect Circle Club Safety Award. Companies awarded employees who demonstrated safety in the workplace. Safety was awarded with items such as plaques, watches, Zippo lighters, ashtrays, and pocketknives.

This photograph from the 1930s shows the Steel Workers Organizing Committee (SWOC) celebrating. The committee was the precursor to the United Steelworkers of America. Throughout the 1900s, unions evolved and played a major role in the daily life of the plant, as well as in the shutdowns of plants across the country. In this photograph, workers hold a sign saying "S.W.O.C. is 90% Strong."

This photograph shows a picket line on February 26, 1941, while a 38-hour strike was in progress at the Lackawanna plant. The strike quickly grew violent when police threw tear gas into the crowds. A quick settlement was reached on the terms that discharged workers could return to work, a grievance procedure would be established, and elections would allow workers to choose their own bargaining representatives.

This Republic Steel advertisement announces employment opportunities, boasting that "800 good jobs are waiting at Republic Steel Corporation." The advertisement goes on to list the departments hiring workers and the benefits offered by the company. It also states, "Apply today for a job with a real postwar future," capitalizing on the euphoric postwar boom years.

Republic Steel's Local 1743 United Steelworkers of America (USWA) post (below) was located at South Park and Bailey Avenues in South Buffalo, close to the Republic plant. Union halls offered a location for union representatives to meet and discuss plant issues and grievances. These halls also served as centers for the communities.

These two photographs were taken in the 1950s at Republic Steel's Local 1743 USWA Union Hall. Officers, members, and guests are seen gathered at the hall. The USWA was formed in the late 1930s, although attempts had been made to unionize steelworkers in the years leading up to its official organization, just before World War II broke out. Unions played a very important role not just in the mills, but also in the community. Religion and politics worked hand in hand with unionization. The union hall in Lackawanna hung the presidential portrait of Pres. John F. Kennedy. Unions were and still are both idolized and feared by society.

Taken in the 1960s, these two photographs show steelworkers in a different environment. Office workers and administrative assistants made up a large percentage of company employees. Western New York's steel industry represented both the blue collar and the white collar. After World War II, Western New York's steelworkers rose out of what is considered the lower-working class and into the growing middle class. Working in a mill was no longer looked down on as "low class." Instead, more steelworkers were supporting middle-class families and first-generation college students than ever before. Steel manufacturers throughout the region offered more diverse employment opportunities throughout their plants.

This photograph shows Bethlehem Steel "loopers" in 1960. Loopers were selected management trainees, including recent college graduates, who "looped" the plant. They worked and studied the management of all the departments before they were placed on the course of management at the Bethlehem Steel Company. The photograph was taken in front of the Administration Building.

This image was taken in the 1960s inside the superintendents' dining room, in the New, or South, Main Office Building at Bethlehem's Lackawanna plant. Superintendents and upper management were salaried employees of the corporation and received a number of benefits. Some of the china seen in this image is now in the Steel Plant Museum's collection.

This photograph, taken on September 20, 1967, shows officials and representatives shaking hands. From left to right are John W. McCann, district representative, United Steelworkers; Robert B. Allen, cochairmen, Bethlehem Steel Group; William H. Harder, president, Buffalo Savings Bank; Roger M. Laible, chairman, Bethlehem Steel Group; and Robert S. Bennett, general manager, Lackawanna plant.

This photograph, taken by Appleton of Buffalo in 1936, shows plant officials touring the strip mill. Directors look on as employees work on the large roll machines. The machines were made by a company called Mesta, a large manufacturer of rolling machinery, whose name is clearly visible on the side of the machine.

Seven

STEEL AND WAR

Industry has forever been impacted by war. The steel industry has seen the influx of production and the effects of postwar prosperity and production decline. During World War I, Buffalo was producing more than 15 million pounds of brass and copper per month. In 1915, J.P. Morgan's firm delivered a $30 million contract to Buffalo Copper & Brass.

Between 1900 and 1920, Lackawanna Steel, New York Steel, and Wickwire Steel employed more than 16,000 Western New Yorkers. Combined, they operated 13 blast furnaces, another 38 open-hearth furnaces, and 20 rolling mills, all of which produced more than two million tons of finished steel products. The 1914 Industrial Census claimed that the local steel industry held a value of more than $23 million, including more than $6 million in wages at more than 250 plants. By 1920, Buffalo was home to 20 large blast furnaces, which used over eight million tons of coke, iron, and limestone in steel production each year.

These numbers would more than double in the wake of World War II. Even before the bombing of Pearl Harbor, the US government was already drawing up defense contracts. Buffalo received over $5 billion in war contracts. Bethlehem Steel, Republic Steel, Wickwire-Spencer, Symington-Gould, Ryerson Steel, and many other companies in the region focused on military production. These companies produced everything from wiring to bolts and other parts used in tanks, planes, and warships.

In 1939, the US government signed a contract with Curtis Wright. In 1940, they employed just over 5,000 people; by 1943, this number had increased to an astonishing 43,000. Around the same time, Bell Aircraft moved to a new plant in Niagara Falls, employing over 30,000 people. In 1944, General Motors employed almost 88,000 Western New Yorkers. At the same time, Bethlehem Steel was manufacturing nearly 10,000 tons of steel a day.

There were more than 450,000 Western New Yorkers in the labor force, earning over $10 million in weekly wages. Production increases and the need for a larger workforce brought more women and minorities into the steel industry than ever before.

`This photograph of the Lackawanna Steel Company's float in a World War I parade in downtown Buffalo was taken in 1917. World War I brought enormous government contracts to the region. This increased demand for industrial production led directly to an influx of workers. The photograph also shows the old public library in the background.

Taken on February 21, 1943, this photograph shows the Bethlehem Steel Company's float in a local parade during World War II. Just beyond the float hangs an advertisement that reads "Buy Bonds." The float boasts that the steel manufactured in Lackawanna helped fight the war at the front. It also lists bars, sheets, and spring steel for machine guns, army trucks, jeeps, and the like.

This World War II–era photograph shows the process of making up the banks of an open-hearth furnace. The workers are shoveling dolomite, which was added to the open-hearth furnace between heats. Dolomite is a rock or mineral containing carbon, magnesium, and calcium that was used as a flux to produce slag.

WORLDS RECORD
"H" BLAST FURNACE
46246 TONS
OCTOBER 1942
LACKAWANNA PLANT
BETHLEHEM STEEL CO

Taken in 1942, this is a photograph of an acknowledgment made by the Bethlehem Steel Company to Lackawanna's blast furnace H. In October of that year, the blast furnace set a world record by producing 46,246 tons. Steel plants throughout the region were producing record-breaking amounts for the war effort.

This photograph from June 18, 1943, shows steelworkers posed in front of an open-hearth building. The photograph reads, "The Brains of #1 OH Labor Gang?" Departments were acknowledged for their accomplishments during the war years. Men who remained in the plant versus serving on the front lines still knew they were contributing.

This 1942 photograph shows the No. 1 open-hearth crew at Bethlehem Steel Company's Lackawanna plant. Many men did remain in the workforce during World War II. Although the historical narrative regarding the steel industry during the war is focused on women entering the mills, many men who did not enlist or did not qualify remained at their posts in the factory.

These two photographs were taken of the Bethlehem Steel Company's Lackawanna plant on June 5, 1942. The images show the ore docks before and after an air raid blackout drill. Seeing what was happening to factories and munitions plants across the globe during wartime, there was an accepted fear that America's plants could be the focus of Axis bombers. With Pearl Harbor fresh in society's mind, air raid drills were practiced throughout the country. Industries, especially those with government-issued war contracts, were increasingly susceptible. With the large amount of wartime manufacturing occurring in the Buffalo area, plants practiced emergency plans and drills on a regular basis to prevent a huge loss of life and manufacturing if an enemy bomber was spotted in the skies overhead.

This photograph was taken on April 21, 1943, at one of the local steel plants. Military officials stop and pose during a tour. Officials often visited and inspected the defense plants that had enormous war contracts, including Bethlehem Steel, Republic Steel, and Wickwire-Spencer Steel.

Pres. Franklin D. Roosevelt was the only sitting president to visit Western New York's steel industry. In this photograph taken on November 2, 1940, during a tour of Western New York's defense industries, well wishers and employees wave and clap as the presidential motorcade exits Bethlehem Steel at gate No. 4 in Lackawanna. President Roosevelt waves his hat from the backseat of the convertible in the foreground.

These photographs, taken during World War II in Lackawanna, show officials (above) and the American Legion Band (below) during two Ships of Victory presentations. The Lackawanna plant received the Maritime "M" Award from the United States Maritime Commission. The commission's shipbuilding program allowed the Lackawanna plant to participate in the production of warships. The two flags are the Maritime "M" pennant and the Victory Fleet flag. Bethlehem's Lackawanna plant received the Maritime award in recognition of its mass production of plates and other steel materials for the Maritime's shipbuilding program. While the Lackawanna plant saw more than 4,200 employees go off to war, those who remained made it possible for the Allied forces to be victorious.

The photograph above shows a Bethlehem Steel employee on a motorcycle on October 30, 1942. The security guard poses with a new company motorcycle used for interplant transportation. The motorcycle was fitting, as it supplied an easy and effective means of maneuvering throughout the massive Lackawanna plant. A company-issued "No Smoking" sign is on the wall of the building behind the guard.

This photograph of two female security guards was taken at the Lackawanna plant on April 14, 1943. When women did enter the workforce at the plant, they were not confined to working in the mills, offices, or mess halls. Many women worked as security guards at the local plants and were known as "pistol-packin' mamas."

1. W. PRINE
2. F. STIEG
3. C. EBENDICK
4. M. HABERER
5. S. KHASZAN
6. J. CLARKE
7. H. BOGNER
8. M. UEBLACKER
9. W. RAPPOLO
10. A. MALECKI
11. W. DURELL
12. G. EVANISKO
13. R. SCHWEICHLER
14. W. KRAUS
15. A. FREITAG
16. A. BESING
17. A. JARDMIN
18. H. HYDE
19. R. COYLE
20. A. SCHAMBERGER
21. R. OSBORNE
22. E. FRANCIS
23. R. DUBARRY

24. G. GREENE
25. F. ECKHARDT
26. E. THOMPSON
27. A. MACKINNON
28. L. DENNIEK
29. W. BORICS
30. B. DION
31. M. KORACH
32. O. GARDOSUICH
33. A. BRUCKLIER
34. M. ALBEE
35.
36. J. JOSEPH
37. M. JONES
38. L. BRUNO (PHOTOGRAPHER)

39. A. MARKMAN (LOST EARLY)
40. G. ALLEIN (" ")

ENG. DEPT. OUTING
CHESTNUT RIDGE PARK

This photograph was taken during Bethlehem Steel Company's engineering outing at Chestnut Ridge Park on July 6, 1944. While the nation and the steel plants were battling the enemy, the men and women who worked there did all they could to escape the depression and austerity of war.

This is the World War II identification badge of Mary Carnevale. Many women were ushered into the steel industry workforce and issued identification badges like this one. Carnevale was employed by the War Department, Army Air Forces Materiel Center. She worked at the United Nations' depot No. 4.

Women began to enter the steel industry's workforce more and more as a result of the outbreak of World War II. Real-life Rosie the Riveters are seen here hard-facing the gears on sprockets. Besides goggles and gloves, the women are wearing very little protective clothing. Instead, they are dressed in their everyday apparel.

This photograph, taken just after the end of World War II, shows two women, one black and one white, working in a Western New York steel plant. The war helped make it more acceptable for women to work in the industry. After the war was over, some women remained in the mills. These two women are unloading refractory bricks from a railway car.

New York governor Thomas E. Dewey visits Republic Steel's Buffalo plant just after the end of World War II. Governor Dewey talks with workers and sees the advancements made by the industry during and after World War II. He served as governor of New York from 1943 to 1954. Dewey, a Republican, ran for president in 1948 but was defeated by incumbent president Harry S. Truman.

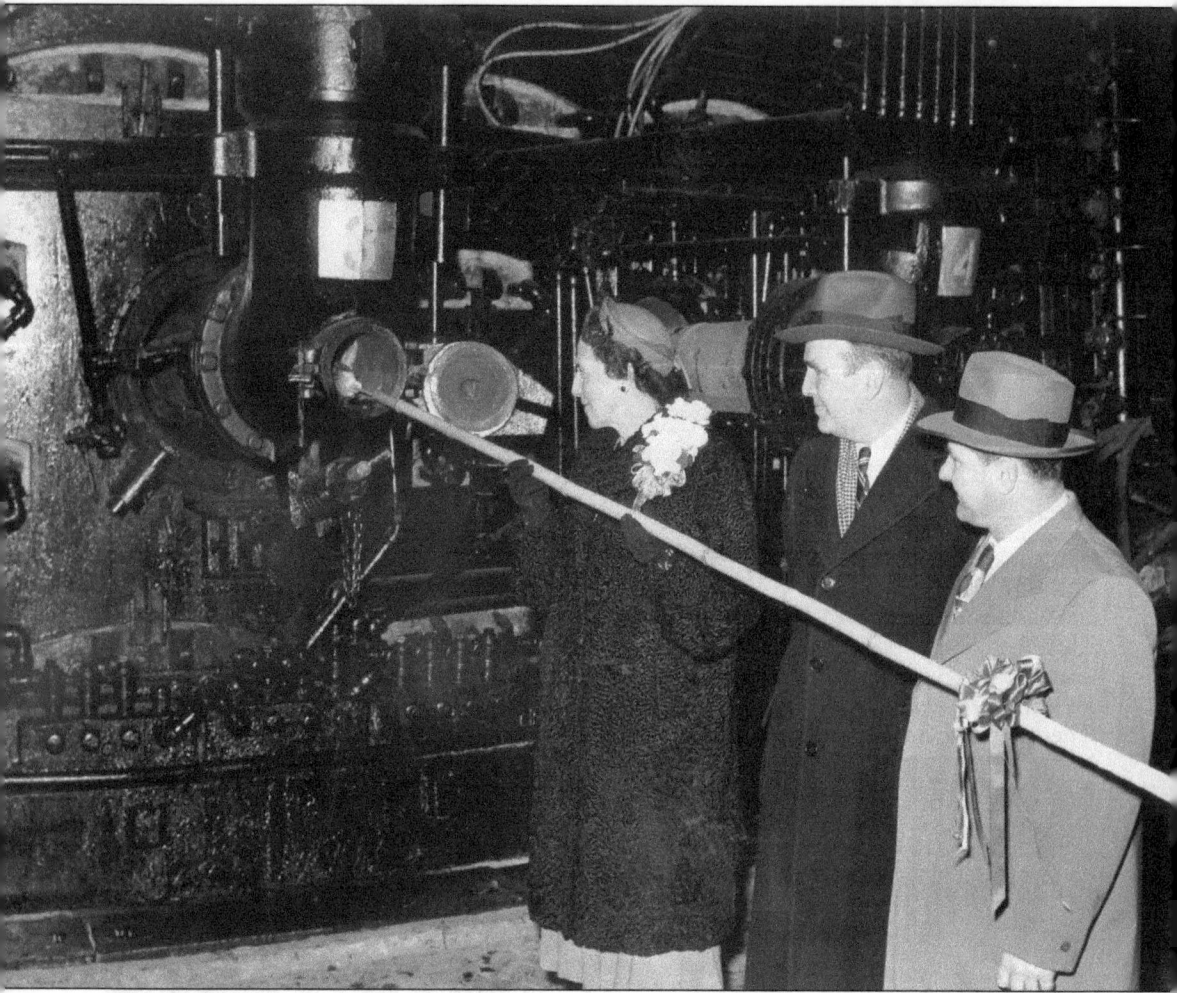

This photograph of Jules Wunsch lighting blast furnace J at Bethehem's Lackawanna plant was taken on March 23, 1952. Wartime profits filled the coffers of the region's steel industry. Bethlehem had earned so much income that it began building new equipment and repairing the old. Wunsch is seen here lighting the brand-new blast furnace J, built during this period of peacetime prosperity. In the years following the war, Bethlehem was buying new plants, building new furnaces, and improving overused ones. Other companies in Western New York were doing the same.

Eight

TIGHTENING THE RUST BELT

During the euphoric post–World War II years, steel companies like Bethlehem took their large war profits on a shopping spree. They built new furnaces, purchased smaller mills, and built new administrative facilities. By the 1970s, older facilities had become obsolete and machinery was in need of upgrading. In 1975, the world steel market had collapsed. This led to an increase in foreign steel imports. By the 1980s, the American steel industry was faltering. At that time, more than 200,000 steel jobs were eliminated, and another 140,000 employees were laid off across the country. Plants were operating at less than 50-percent capacity while imported steel made up more than 25 percent of steel sold in the United States.

Wickwire-Spencer Steel closed its plant just north of Buffalo in 1963, then a subsidiary of Colorado Fuel and Iron (CF&I). Tonawanda Iron & Steel was shut down in 1971 and demolished by 1974. By 1976, the Allegheny-Ludlum plant in Dunkirk changed hands. The Lackawanna plant closed its doors in 1982, and Bethlehem filed for bankruptcy in 2001.

The final indignity came in 2013, when the former Administration Building was demolished by its owners following a long and emotional legal battle with preservationists. Some former steelworkers saw it as a sore reminder of an industry that collapsed under their feet and crushed their idyllic world, wanting it razed in order to extinguish bitter memories. Others wanted to see the building saved for posterity's sake, in the hopes that the important history of Western New York's steel industry would be saved and preserved for the benefit of future generations.

Today, the United States is the third-largest producer of steel, following China and Japan. Companies like Ryerson Steel, Dresser-Rand, Alcas-Cutco, and Atlas Steel still operate throughout Western New York, along with smaller manufacturing plants. However, the region's steel industry will never be the same. Most of what was Bethlehem Steel has been demolished. All that remains of Republic Steel is a large, grassy brown field on South Park Avenue. The time has come for the community to celebrate the legacy of the once-mighty steel industry and preserve the legacy left behind.

This aerial view of the Bethlehem Steel Company's Lackawanna plant was taken in 1964. Western New York's steel industry climaxed in the 1950s and 1960s during the era of postwar prosperity. By the 1970s, the industry had plateaued. Soon, this would lead to an unstoppable downward spiral caused by excessive costs, lack of demand, and foreign competition.

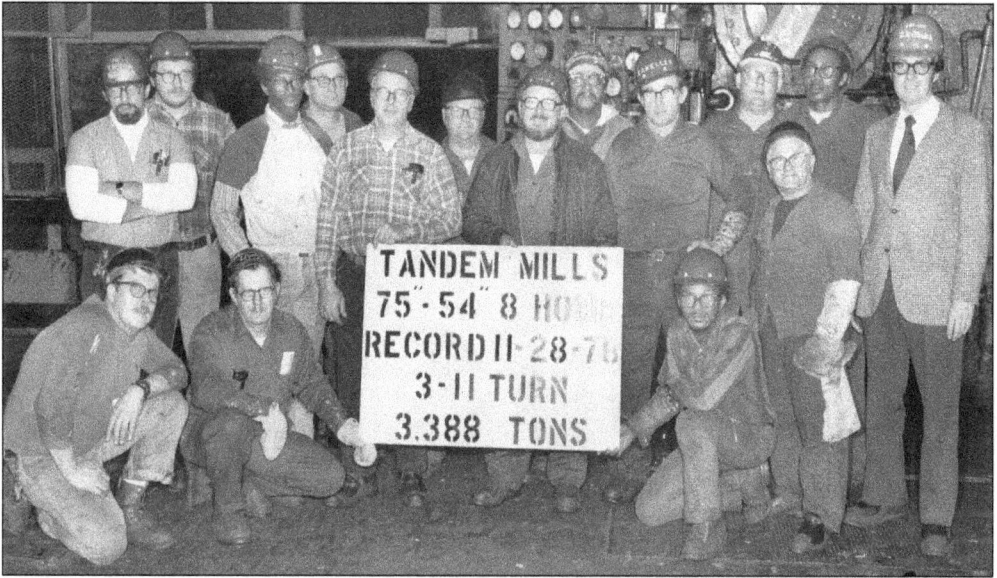

This 1978 photograph shows a new record set by the tandem mills at the Lackawanna plant. A tandem mill was a modern way of making sheet steel and differed from previous methods used by traditional rolling mills. Before, steel would be passed through the mill several times to achieve a specified gauge. The tandem mill broke this process down to one pass. Tandems could be hot or cold rolling mills.

This photograph shows the construction of Bethlehem Steel's galvanizing plant in Lackawanna. Constructed at the cost of $20 million in 1962, the mill was located on the south side of Route 5, across from the main plant property. Galvanized steel was a specialized product manufactured to meet customers' specified needs. The former galvanized mill building is now owned by Metalico, a metal recycling company.

This photograph of Bethlehem employees was taken at the galvanize mill in Lackawanna on December 22, 1981. Bethlehem claimed that the galvanize mill in Lackawanna was the largest in the nation. After the plant closings of the 1980s, the galvanize mill was one the last surviving Bethlehem plants in Western New York.

This photograph was taken at the No. 5 cold strip mill, or skin mill, in 1956. The image shows a worker feeding the mill at the entry end, looking northwest. Cold roll sheets can be manufactured at a number of different gauges. "Skin-rolled" refers to the thickness of the finished product. Skin rolling reduces the steel sheet thickness only slightly, whereas "full-hard" reduces the thickness of the steel by about 50 percent.

A worker puts the final touches on a rolled steel coil at the Lackawanna plant in the 1970s. Once sheet steel had completed the manufacturing process, including the rolling and galvanizing processes, it was checked for imperfections by a metallurgist and then bound tightly. Each coil was then lifted into the coil storage area and inventoried before it was shipped to its final destination.

This photograph, taken at the Bethlehem Steel Company's Lackawanna plant, shows workers preparing galvanized sheet products for shipping. Packaging tags hanging from the steel read, "Made in the U.S.A." These steel sheets were delivered to customers who then used them in the manufacturing of other products.

This artist's rendering from around 1930 shows Bethlehem Steel's Lackawanna plant, with special emphasis on the structural fabricating shop. Structural fabricating allowed Bethlehem to manufacture materials for construction and other pieces according to customer specifications. When Bethlehem Steel took over the Lackawanna Steel Company, it doubled its manufacturing

STRUCTURAL FABRICATING SHOP

abilities, built new mills, and created more departments. The plant quickly became the epitome of steel manufacturing in Western New York. Soon, the plant's employment numbers skyrocketed from thousands to tens of thousands. The plant was diversified by the ethnic enclaves that immigrated and migrated to the region, all clamoring for jobs offered by this and other mills.

These photographs, taken in the 1960s, show the structural shipping yard at the Lackawanna plant. The photograph above shows the 48-inch rotary straightener at the roll build up area. The image below shows the shipping yard, where specialty products are being finished and bundled to make ready for transport. Structural steel usually refers to products such as I-beams and other similar products used in construction. Bethlehem Steel is famous for several building projects, including the Golden Gate Bridge and the Empire State Building. Many of these later products were used in smaller construction projects throughout the country.

These photographs, taken in 1970, show the structural shipping yard at the Lackawanna plant. Here, structural shapes that built the nation's buildings and bridges would wait to be delivered to their final destination after they were produced and inspected. In 1954, Western New York boasted almost 200,000 manufacturing jobs. By 1967, this number had fallen to around 150,000. Economic crisis loomed large by the 1970s for the region's steel and automobile industries. In 1971, Bethlehem Steel permanently laid off half of its 18,000 employees at the Lackawanna plant. Western New York was no longer a major producer of steel.

This photograph, taken at Bethlehem's Lackawanna plant in 1961, shows an employee "scarfing" steel billets at the steel preparation billet yard. Scarfing was the process of removing defective layers of blooms and slabs in order to prepare the steel for rolling.

Taken in the 1960s, this photograph shows the Peddinghaus Bender Line. Peddinghaus was a major manufacturer of structural steel fabricating equipment. These workers are making steel rods at the Lackawanna plant. Behind the worker in the center, a safety sign hangs from the wall that reads, "Can You Afford an Accident."

Taken in 1975, this photograph shows the pouring of steel at a basic oxygen furnace. Many of the steel companies had become obsolete by this time. Manufacturers were using outdated equipment and could not compete with the smaller domestic and foreign mills that were manufacturing the same quality products at cheaper prices.

This 1950s photograph shows the construction of the New Main, or South, Main Office Building in Lackawanna. The site was the former Bethlehem Steel employee gardens. The building still stands near Woodlawn Beach, where Milestrip Road meets Route 5 at the south edge of the former Lackawanna plant. Today, the building is known as the Gateway Building and serves as a reminder of the industry's postwar boom.

Taken after a snowstorm in 1963, this photograph shows the ravages of winter at the New Main Office Building at the Lackawanna plant. Winter weather did little to deter the steel industry until the great Blizzard of 1977. In January 1977, Western New York had already received almost 14 feet of snow before it was blasted with 70-mile-per-hour winds for three straight days. Workers were trapped at the plant. No one was severely injured, but the snow stopped production and cost the company $10 million. This was an all-around bad year for Bethlehem, which was already facing a financial crisis. Mother Nature gave Bethlehem another run for its money later that same year when a flood in Johnstown, Pennsylvania, crippled Bethlehem's operations at that plant.

This photograph shows the Administration Building in Lackawanna around 1970. Already the symbol of Western New York's steel industry, the building began to feel the effects of the economic crisis in the 1970s. The building had become outdated and in desperate need of restoration after administrative operations had been removed to the New Main Office Building, at the opposite end of the plant.

This photograph from the 1970s shows Dresser employees at the Depew plant. In 1880, Solomon R. Dresser founded the Dresser Company in Bradford, Pennsylvania, manufacturing coupling pipe sections. That same year, the Clark Company was founded in Belmont, New York, manufacturing agricultural machinery. In 1912, the Clark Company burned to the ground and a new factory was constructed in Olean, New York. In 1938, the Clark Brothers Company merged with S.R. Dresser. In 1968, Dresser Industries purchased the former Symington-Wayne Corporation (previously the Symington-Gould Company) in Depew to form the Dresser Transportation Division. The Gould Coupler, a revolutionary railway connector for rolling stock, was made at the Gould Coupler Company in Depew since the 1880s. In 1924, the Gould Company was purchased by the Symington Company and it became the Symington-Gould Company. Dresser's Depew plant closed in 1985. In 1987, Dresser Industries, as it was then known, combined with Ingersoll-Rand to form the Dresser-Rand Company. Although this company has locations worldwide, operations in Olean continue today, manufacturing engine and machinery products. Dresser-Rand is one of the largest employers in the Olean area.

This photograph from around 1980 shows the main entrance to Republic Steel, on South Park Avenue in South Buffalo. Over the years, several thousand men and women went through this gate to work. Although struggling, Republic remained in operation in the 1970s and produced structural steel, like beams and bars. The mill operated two blast furnaces through the 1970s and also used an articulated mill line. However, the lack of more modern and updated equipment limited Republic's production abilities. Competitors both at home and abroad were quickly outproducing them. The plant was slowly shut down until 1984, when it was finally closed for good. That same year, Republic was merged into Jones & Laughlin Steel, a subsidiary of the Ling, Temco & Vought Corporation, or LTV. In 2000, LTV filed for bankruptcy. The Buffalo plant was already closed, and thousands of employees were out of work.

Taken in the 1980s, this photograph shows Hanna Furnace after it was closed and abandoned. In 1982, Donner-Hanna Coke, located at Mystic and Abby Streets, also ceased operations. The Hanna Furnace Corporation, which had operated at full capacity in the 1930s despite the Great Depression, was no more. Today, there is nothing remaining of the company. The Union Ship Canal has been cleaned and beautified as a park.

Taken in the 1980s, this photograph shows what was left after the demolition of Hanna Furnace. Its once-great blast furnaces that reached toward the sky came down in only a few weeks. On the south side of the canal, a few small, hilly mounds in the earth cover blast furnace bases like this one. They are the only memory left of Hanna Furnace on the canal.

Taken in 1995, this photograph shows the demolition of a basic oxygen furnace at Bethlehem's Lackawanna plant. In 1982, it was announced that Bethlehem would cut 7,300 jobs at the Lackawanna plant. Just 15 years later, most of the operations that had been mothballed by Bethlehem were demolished. Today, most of the plant is open space. In 2012, it was announced that the empty lots would become an industrial park.

This photograph shows the demolition of blast furnace J at the Lackawanna plant, on September 13, 1986. Although the blast furnaces at the Lackawanna plant are no more, the original stone blast furnaces for the Lackawanna Iron & Steel Company still stand preserved near Scranton, Pennsylvania. They remain as a reminder of the once-powerful steel industry, which evolved, climaxed, and disintegrated in less than 150 years.

This photograph was taken at the Lackawanna plant on September 24, 1988. Taken from what was known as Times Square, it looks north through the plant toward the blast furnaces. Times Square was a main intersection in the plant and was always busy with foot and transport traffic. During shift changes, the mill turned into a heavily congested city. This image shows the devastation wreaked on the plant during its deconstruction. The Lackawanna property once boasted 1,300 acres. Now, most of this land is dormant and unusable due to pollution and overuse. Even after Bethlehem Steel closed its Lackawanna plant, some pieces of it were reorganized and operated by other companies. This would not last long, however, and most of the plant remains vacant. There is hope that the land can be used for future development.

This 1980s photograph shows strip mill employee Mel Pawlak (left) and Walter Williams at the Lackawanna plant. Williams became president of the Bethlehem Steel Corporation in 1986 and was credited with trying to salvage the sinking ship that was Bethlehem. Although he was able to prevent the impending demise of the company, and even improve sales and stock prices for a time, it was short-lived and could not last. When Williams retired in 1992, he said that the downsizing that occurred during his time as chairman put the company on the road of recovery. That recovery, however, never occurred. Williams has as many critics as he does fans. In the mid-to-late 1980s, he was able to hold back the plant from going bankrupt for a few more years.

This photograph was taken at a retirement party at a basic oxygen furnace in 1977. By then, most steel mills in Western New York had downsized and some had even closed. Retirement was often bittersweet for steelworkers, as many loved and hated their jobs at the same time. This was especially true for the impending hardships that would come in the 1980s. Bethlehem Steel was paying billions of dollars into the pension funds of over 95,000 former employees. The overall pension plan was only 45 percent funded, including assets and liabilities. When it finally went bankrupt, the company's pension was taken over by the Pension Guaranty Benefit Corporation, a federal agency. In 2002, the steel industry accounted for 50 percent of all claims against the agency. When Bethlehem filed for bankruptcy, it was $4.5 billion in debt, or $300 million more than the company's total assets.

BETHLEHEM
STEEL
PLANT

BUFFALO 1984

SCALE

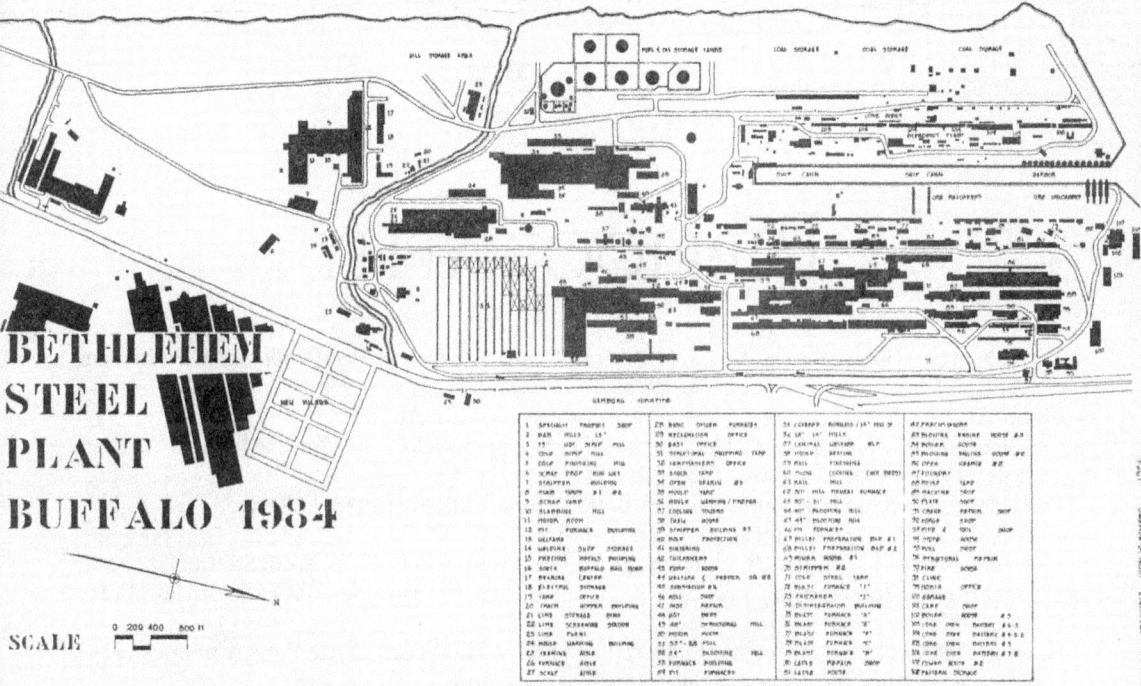

This is a blueprint of Bethlehem Steel Company's Lackawanna plant in 1984. The company had turned the former Lackawanna Steel Company into a powerhouse of steelmaking, increasing numbers across the board. However, the American steel industry was collapsing. Most of the buildings featured on this map are no more. By the time this map was drawn, steel production in the region was shut down with the exception of a few basic steel manufacturing mills and subsidiaries. As the manufacturers shut their doors across Western New York, the community felt the effects almost overnight. Service businesses like restaurants and retailers were forced to close, and venerable institutions faced bankruptcy. Buffalo suffered a mass exodus of its citizens, who left seeking better opportunities in cities that offered employment, specifically in the west and along the coasts.

BIBLIOGRAPHY

Bethlehem Steel Corporation. *The Properties and Plants of Bethlehem Steel Corporation*. Bethlehem, PA: Bethlehem Steel Corporation, 1925.

Garn, Andrew. *Bethlehem Steel*. New York: Princeton Architectural Press, 1999.

Goldman, Mark. *High Hopes: The Rise and Decline of Buffalo, New York*. Albany, NY: State University of New York Press, 1983.

Hill, Henry Wayland, ed. *Municipality of Buffalo, New York: A History 1720–1923*, Vol. II. New York: Lewis Historical Publishing Company, Inc., 1923.

Howell, Thomas R., William A. Noellert, Jesse G. Kreier, and Alan Wm. Wolf. *Steel and the State: Government Intervention and Steel's Structural Crisis*. Boulder, CO: Westview Press, Inc., 1988.

Koenig, Stephen M. *South Buffalo Railway*. David City, NE: South Platte Press; Columbia, MO: Brueggenjohann/Reese, Inc., 2004.

"Lackawanna Plant: Bethlehem Steel Corporation." *Lackawanna Plant Newsletter*.

"Lackawanna Plant Celebrates 75 Years of Steelmaking." *People 'N Steel: Lackawanna Plant Newsletter*, reprint, 1979.

Langan, Michael D. *Tapped Out: A Worker's Memoir of Bethlehem Steel's Rise and Demise in Western New York*. Buffalo, NY: Bates Jackson, 2010.

Leary, Thomas E. and Elizabeth C. Sholes. *From Fire to Rust: Business, Technology and Work at the Lackawanna Steel Plant, 1899–1983*. Buffalo, NY: Buffalo and Erie County Historical Society, 1987.

The Morning Call. *Forging America: The Story of Bethlehem Steel*. Philadelphia, PA: The Morning Call, 2010.

Savage, Philip S. *The Story of Donner-Hanna Coke Corporation, Buffalo, N.Y. 1917–1956: A Unique Corporate Partnership Based on Faith in One's Associates*. Buffalo, NY: Donner-Hanna Coke Corporation, 1956.

Sikorskyj, Jerod J. and Jonathan W. Senchyne. *Living Forge: The Rust Belt Rises – The Literary and Arts Journal of the Rust Belt*. Buffalo, NY: Living Forge, Inc., 2004.

Taylor, Henry Louis Jr., ed. *African Americans and the Rise of Buffalo's Post-Industrial City, 1940 to Present*, Vol. II. Buffalo, NY: Buffalo Urban League, Inc., 1990.

Strohmeyer, John. *Crisis in Bethlehem: Big Steel's Battle to Survive*. Bethesda, MD: Adler & Adler Publishers, Inc., 1986.

ABOUT THE STEEL PLANT MUSEUM OF WESTERN NEW YORK

The Steel Plant Museum was formed in 1984 under the coordination of Jerry Soltis, a Bethlehem Steel employee, and James Swinnich, a museum professional. Originally housed in the basement of the Lackawanna Public Library, on Ridge Road in Lackawanna, the museum quickly became a haven for objects and archives that were saved from the former Bethlehem Steel plant. It soon became a memorial to the entire industry that was lost in Buffalo and the Western New York region.

Over the years, former workers and their families helped build a collection of artifacts, archives, photographs, and art. It was formally organized with a board of directors and a board of trustees, and acted as a place for former workers and their families to visit, volunteer, and support.

In 2003, the museum applied for a charter from the New York State Board of Regents. It received a provisional five-year charter on July 21, 2005. In 2013, it received its permanent charter, becoming the Steel Plant Museum of Western New York (SPMWNY). By 2009, the museum collection had grown exponentially and shared storage space at the library and at a church, while still having pieces scattered about the region. In 2010, SPMWNY was offered rental space recently purchased by the Western New York Railway Historical Society (WNYRHS) at 100 Lee Street in South Buffalo. In 2011, the museum reopened its doors at the Heritage DiscoveRY Center (also known as HDC; the "RY" is capitalized to refer to railway). One day, this former industrial site will become a 35-acre rail and industrial museum.

The new HDC location allows significant expansion of exhibits and archival space. Future plans include additional expansion at the HDC site and working with the WNYRHS and other historic preservation groups to create an attractive tourist destination. Since its move, the organization has received a great deal of press and community involvement and has been utilized by tour groups, scholars, and researchers.

The mission of SPMWNY is to preserve the history of the steel industry in Western New York, through collecting, studying, and interpreting artifacts and archives that reflect our industrial past, present, and future. For more information, please visit the museum's website, www.steelplantmuseumwny.org.

Visit us at
arcadiapublishing.com

....

www.ingramcontent.com/pod-product-compliance
Lightning Source LLC
Chambersburg PA
CBHW050611110426
42813CB00008B/2521